44
Winning Tactics
for Great Soccer
Goalkeeping

Mirsad Hasic

DEDICATION

I dedicate this book to my wife.

CONTENTS

ACKNOWLEDGMENTS

I would like to thank my family for their support.

Introduction

This book, "44 Winning Tactics for Great Soccer Goalkeeping," is a complimentary to my first book "44 Soccer Goalie Mistakes to Avoid." The latter is by far one of the best – if not THE best – books to cover the topic of goalkeeping from A to Z.

The majority of goalkeeping books nowadays tend to be too impersonal and too presumptuous. Many are full of academic, tedious information that doesn't teach goalkeepers anything new.

In fact, a lot of the content in these books appears copied and rehashed. This is not my style. This book, along with "44 Soccer Goalie Mistakes to Avoid," covers new areas of goalkeeping.

Here I explain things in an easy-to-understand and entertaining way. Any of you who are familiar with my work will know that my approach is quite different from most others.

I, We, and You…

You will notice throughout this book how I write in the first person "I" quite a lot. This is deliberate. It is to make your journey more interesting and the reading experience less pressuring.

There are just too many coldly-written soccer books on sale today, and that's one approach I make sure to avoid. The "I" accounts in this book are more likely to get your focus too. This is because you will relate to some of the things I write about on a more personal level.

I also use "we" on occasions as well. This is because I have been where you are at now, at least to some extent. This helps me to relate to what you're going through, meaning we're in this together. My personal approach lets you to pick up on similarities so much easier.

I also use the "you" approach because I'm addressing you, my reader, directly.

Inside "44 Winning Tactics for Great Soccer Goalkeeping" you will find a treasure-trove of helpful information. This book covers not only the physical, but also the mental side of a great goalkeeping.

It explains, in detail, how the best of the best goalkeepers reached their greatness. You will learn what they did and how they did it. You will undoubtedly be able to apply some of these ideas to your own game.

The style of this book is one of "serious fun." It's "serious" because I want you to succeed, and it's "fun" because without that there is no point. I am certain that these chapters will encourage you to read this book from cover to cover. I am confident that you will want to get to work and apply many of the tips, advice and drills into your own game ASAP.

Why Goalkeepers Fail

There are many goalkeepers around today who are tall, strong and ambitious. On the face of it, they have all the physical traits that a keeper needs to become successful. Alas, not so many of them ever make it into professional soccer. Why?

The answer is simple. Despite having the physical attributes and talent, they lack the right knowledge. In other words, they are ill-informed and/or misguided. They have what it takes, yet they are missing the knowhow of how to exploit their own talents.

Most of these guys also have the wrong mentality or mindset to help them progress past a certain point. Well, it is the purpose of this book to show you what to do, and equally as important, what NOT to do.

You will also get to learn how to develop that "winning attitude," which is essential for succeeding. Forming a successful mindset will be a game changer.

Once you get to change the way you view things, the things you view will change accordingly – and for the better. This is something that will not only improve your goalkeeping abilities. Developing a new attitude and outlook will also help you to become successful in many other areas of your life too.

Here's what to expect from this book:

- Learn the 44 things that all great goalkeepers did to become successful. From Peter Schmeichel to Manuel Neuer, this book covers everything.
- The one thing that you need to become physically fitter, so that you can last longer on the field.
- The situations when you have to come out of your goal. Learn what to do, and how to do them, whenever you`re out of the box.
- How to catch the ball the professional way, without letting it fall on the ground, and without hurting yourself through wrong moves.
- The best way to throw a ball, along with when and how to choose the right type of throws to match the situations.
- How to become fearful and intimidating to the opposition. Plus, how to create an effect on your opponents that makes them soft around you.

- How to behave – specifically - when dealing with penalty kicks, and the four things you must do to greatly improve your chances of saving penalty shots.
- How to become expert at punts and how to transform yourself into a punting machine that starts impressive counterattacks for your teammates.
- How to deal with passes coming to you from your teammates, especially when being pressured by an opponent. Learn how to successfully kick the ball away, instead of giving your opponents an easy opportunity to score against you.
- How to become a leader on the field. Know when and how to communicate effectively with your teammates in different situations during the game.
- Learn the three commandments that you should follow in order to become a master at saving free kicks.
- Find out what the correct dive is and how to fully use your physical capabilities to save up to eight times as many shots at your goal as you are currently used to.
- Discover the one thought and act that will catapult your success to stratospheric levels when followed through on.
- How to save fouls given against you inside the penalty area. Find out how not to get distracted by the fact that eight out of each ten fouls of this type are transformed into goals.

- Learn when and how to play headers to best effect, and how to make yourself "complete" as a goalie, like the German keeper, Manuel Neuer.
- How to catch corners like never before, and the six things you should follow in order to become a cross master.
- How to use both your legs and your hands equally and to best effect, like all the great goalkeepers.
- How to avoid the silliest of mistakes. The type of blunders that can break a goalkeeper's career in an instant.
- Identify the mistakes that amateur goalkeepers make when standing between the two bars. These are the things that lead to very easy goals when gone unnoticed.
- How to stay motivated and hungry for the entire duration of the game. Learn also, of the secret behind why many of the great goalkeepers last so long in their soccer careers.
- Understand bouncing balls better, and know exactly how you should train in practice to master these better (I have two drills that will make you an expert in no time).
- Discover what the right position is to take in front of the goal line for you to save a maximum number of balls. Find out how to position yourself inside the penalty area so that you can cope with any change in both the direction and speed of the ball.

- Know what to study about your opponents in a way that lets you exploit most of their tricks, strengths and weaknesses during the game.
- Learn how to deal with deflections and the exercises you must perform so that you can save the majority of them.
- Know the difference between playing in different weather conditions. Learn how to adapt your style of play for windy, rainy or sunny days.
- Discover the one single mistake to avoid so that you don`t blame yourself when the game is over. This is a serious trap that many goalkeepers fall in to, and one that can often see their downfall.
- Know what to do when your team is leading in the score. Learn how to use your goalkeeper privileges to control the tempo of the game.
- Learn how to maintain your focus when an opponent tries to mess with you using inappropriate actions or words, and most importantly, know how to get him punished for it.
- Discover the one trick that all strikers do in breakaways. Find out how to avoid giving the striker what he wants in these situations.
- Recognize what to do so that your saves don't go in vain (these simple mistakes can, and often do, wash away goalkeeper's efforts in a nanosecond).

- Find out why confidence is so important, and learn of the scientific way to further build your own self-confidence. After reading this chapter you WILL definitely get to improve your own self-assurance.
- Know what drills you should master in order to have extremely fast reflexes. Speed is a must-have skill if you are serious about becoming a great goalkeeper.
- Learn how to enhance all your mental powers the night before the game. This will assure you are well-prepared to perform at your very best level when the game is on.
- Discover how to become fearless inside the box and how to stop fearing hurt or injury when the game is on (when left to run rampant, fear can disrupt a goalkeeper's performance like nothing else).
- The importance of warming up. Learn how to warm up like a pro. Understand what you should do before the game starts. This will enable you to use all your physical capabilities to best effect once the game commences.
- Realize how to embrace mistakes and make every single one count in your favor. Discover the ways that will let you exploit your mistakes and make your performance 10 times better in just six months.

You will learn about all of these things and more besides from this one book. Follow the suggestions and guidance in these chapters and you will develop into the goalkeeper that you have always aspired to be.

1. Staying Fit

A common misconception, when it comes to goalkeepers, is that they don't have to be as fit as the field players. The thinking behind this is that keepers run around a lot less than their teammates.

They also have a lot of rest periods whenever the ball is on the other side of the field. These are the simple facts.

So it's understandable to see why people might think that keeper's don't need to be as fit as field players. Despite this, it is still a misconception to suggest that a goalie doesn't have to work on his fitness levels in the same way as the other players.

The reality is that a goalkeeper must be just as fit - if not fitter - than the field players. And for a keeper to reach the required levels of fitness he must excel in several different areas too.

A goalkeeper must be able to exert a great deal of energy in a very short period of time. He needs to do this at the drop of a hat, and perform with razor sharp reflexes at a moment's notice.

Let's look at other situations where a goalie needs to be super fit.

The Sprinter

Goalkeepers must be physically prepared to sprint many times throughout any game. Sometimes, these sprints will last for short intervals. Other times he may have to sprint for much longer periods.

The keeper never knows when the next attack will be. In some cases they can be relentless, coming in one after another. A "reasonably fit" keeper would never be able to keep up.

Quick Witted and Powerful

There is another aspect of goalkeeping that requires you to exert a high level of energy in a short period of time. It is when those rebound shots happen, as they invariably do. Here you must have enough energy to get up fast, assess the situation quick, and throw yourself back into the moment. You never quite know when you might need to make a second or third save in rapid succession.

If you save a shot, and there is a rebound, you must get up as fast and try to stop the next attempt. And the next one; and the one after that, as the case may be.

When that ball is in the keeper's domain, the danger is unpredictable. The attacks can, and quite often are, ruthless. Quick-thinking and fast-acting are necessary traits of a good goalkeeper.

To play like this a goalie not only needs to be super-fit but he must be strong too. He also has to be very quick on his feet.

Why Goalies Need Strength

You can be unfit but still strong. A goalkeeper, however, needs both strength and fitness if he's to excel in his position. This is not the type of strength that displays bulging muscles either. In fact, too much muscle would be a hindrance rather than a help to a goalkeeper.

Expanded chests and massive arms would only weaken his performance. This would be especially evident when compared to a keeper who has gymnastic or athletic strengths and capabilities.

A goalkeeper can be lean, well-toned, and incredibly strong when he works on his body the right way. Having good physical strength is more important for keepers than it is for field players. Anyone who played both in goal and out on the field will know this.

Leg Strength

There are a number of ways where strength comes to the rescue when trying to become a great goalkeeper. Let's look first at leg strength. Having strong legs enables you to kick the ball harder and further, jump higher, and dive faster. Sturdy legs also help prevent against injury whenever a player tackles you or hits your legs hard in some way.

Upper Body Strength

Having good upper-body and core strength helps when challenging forwards for crosses in the air. It's also useful for challenging forwards on the ground, during breakaways.

Arm Strength

Having excellent arm strength helps you to throw the ball much further. Moreover, hand and finger strength helps you send the ball away with more control and power when stopping powerful shots.

The Importance of Agility

An agile goalkeeper is quicker and more flexible than one who is not agile. When you are fit, you become more agile naturally. A high level of agility is crucial for any goalkeeper.

In fact, soccer agility drills should be part of his usual training routine. Having exceptional agility means having the ability to change direction and speed in an instant. Any keeper who is agile and has an acute sense of anticipation is a blessing to his team.

Goalkeepers are often required to move from side to side across their goal area during a game. Once again, being agile helps a lot here too. Situations where the goalie has to move around a lot occur when opponents switch the point of attack.

There are times when the keeper needs to shuffle quickly across the goal to stop a shot going into a corner. There are plenty of situations that dictate sudden switches of movements for the goalie. These circumstances all need excellent footwork, which is a component of agility.

Changing direction quickly is a part of agility, and in turn a part of fitness. If you can learn how to change direction fast it will be a huge advantage to you and your team. Speed and accuracy is always of the essence for good goalkeeping. Both speed and accuracy require high and consistent levels of fitness and strength.

To put this all into some kind of perspective, consider the following situation:

You are six yards off your line and waiting for a shot. This shot is coming in from the opposing team's forward and it's high.

OK, you know it's going over you, so you have to act fast to try and save it. First, you have to change direction quickly, which is where agility comes in. Then, you have to backpedal as fast as you can, and without tripping.

To do this requires good footwork, which is also part of agility. To finish off you need to jump high, and the stronger your legs are the higher you will be able to jump.

Finally, you need good arm, hand, and finger strength so that you can play with enough power to send the ball over the bar.

As you can see from the scenario above, all the important aspects of good goalkeeping come into play. There is fitness, strength, quick-wit, and agility.

2. Think Inside the Box

One of the less obvious mistakes a goalkeeper makes is by not coming off his goal line when in fact he should do.

It's easy to tell when a goalkeeper messes up when an easy shot rolls through his legs, or if he misjudges a cross. It is harder to tell whether a goalkeeper is at fault based on the fact that he didn't come out, even though he probably should have done.

A big mistake that many amateur goalkeepers make is to believe that staying on the goal line is by far their best position. They think that this is the only place to save all shots and catch all balls. They are wrong. There are many situations where this is the worst possible place for them to be. Fear is probably the reason for their belief, even though they might not see it like that.

There is a misunderstanding that suggests moving from the goal line leaves the goalmouth empty and exposed. It becomes a wide open opportunity for the other team's shots and headers, the keeper assumes.

In other words, inexperienced goalies see this as an open invitation for the rival side to score. There are many situations where they are so wrong in their assumptions, much to their detriment.

This is the type of mistake that is so huge that it holds back progress. Those keepers who believe that leaving the goal line is a bad idea are the ones who will never reach their full potential.

If you can relate to this, then you have to change your thinking if you want to excel as a goalie. That means you need to adjust the way you play in goal.

For you to realize the importance of frequently coming away from your goal line, you first need to understand the reasons why you must do it. There are in fact several advantages to coming outside the box. Let's take a look at each of them in turn.

By coming out of your goal line you are doing three things. The first is to cut off the angles and cover a wider area of the goal.

The second is to advance on the rival team's attacker before he makes his move. And the third is to intercept the ball and prevent dangerous counter attacks from reaching your penalty area.

None of these things is achievable by standing on the goal line, waiting for the action to come to you.

Cutting off the Angle

Let's start by looking at the importance of cutting off the angle. By coming out of the box you are blocking the goal. This gives the player taking the shot less goal to fire at. You are also making the goal appear as a smaller target to your opponent.

When faced with a breakaway situation, if you come out and position yourself well, you then become a lot bigger than the goal. The forward sees you coming toward him, which he will likely find intimidating. This may force him to make a move he wasn't prepared for. And it's not just a breakaway situation that you have to leave your goal for.

Know that whenever you take a few steps away from your goal before taking a dive, you are doing yourself, and your team, a huge favor. This is because the area you have to cover to catch the ball, or to clear it away, decreases as a direct result of you advancing away from the goal line.

Try this yourself:

Stand right on the goal line and make a dive, as if going after a ball that's heading toward the upper corner of the goal. Once you've done that, go back to the goal line and advance two or three forward. Now attempt to save the same imaginary ball. Now compare these two dives with each other.

You should come to realize how you cover more goal space whenever you advance a little away from your goal line before making the dive.

Advance on the Attacker

This leads us to the second advantage of cutting off the angle. Here we force the player holding the ball in the breakaway to make a move. What this does is prevent him from shooting from his preferred scoring angle, and at the time he wanted to strike.

By you coming out of the goal, the forward has one of three options. He can shoot right away, he can pass the ball on to another player, or he can try to take the ball around you. None of these options was likely to have been his preference as he approached the goal.

By coming away from your goal line you force the opponent into a situation where he has to make a snap decision. You have just made things a lot harder for him by adding to his pressure. This would not have happened if you had waited patiently on your goal line, anticipating his shot.

Intercept the Ball

The third advantage of coming out of the box is to prevent an attack from happening. You have two options here. The first is to get the ball from the forward's feet with your hands. The second is to play as a sweeper-keeper.

You have to ready yourself, as a keeper, to race out and grab the ball if the forward makes a large touch on it. If you stay on your goal line, well, the forward can take as many big touches as he wants and get away with it.

In other words, you are allowing him to control the situation. You must not let this happen. As soon as you see him flounder your job is to ambush the ball.

Another way to prevent danger is by clearing the ball away from the forward's feet. The German goalkeeper, Manuel Neuer, has epitomized this strategy in recent years.

In fact, Neuer is excellent at playing the role of sweeper-keeper. For those who are unfamiliar with the term, a sweeper-keeper describes a goalkeeper who almost doubles as a center back.

The name comes about when the goalie willingly leaves his 18 yard box to clear the ball away with his feet. Neuer is the perfect sweeper-keeper.

He has been able to prevent many threatening situations from developing by playing in this manner. This is the most complex part of coming out from the goal area. To be a good sweeper-keeper means you must have good speed and perfect timing.

If you mess up outside the 18 yard box, the forward can take the ball around you and get a clear shot at an empty goal.

If you mess up from inside the 18 yard box, the forward can still take the ball around. However, in the latter situation, he may end up taking the ball too far and lose the advantage of a good shooting angle.

When clearing the ball away with your feet, your main aim is to send it as far away as possible. The last thing you want to do is deliver it back to the feet of another opponent. To summarize this chapter:

Thinking only inside of the box is a big mistake. It gives any forward an advantage because he has plenty of time to think and prepare his plan of attack. By staying inside the box means you don't get to cut off the angles.

Nor do you get to make yourself appear bigger to approaching opponents. And finally, by remaining inside the box you won't be able to prevent attacks from developing.

3. Develop a Good Goalkeeper Stance

One of the most basic principles of a successful goalkeeper is to develop a good goalkeeper stance. And once you have it, you have to maintain it, in both practice and games. In other words, it becomes a natural part of who you are. It should not be something that you have to consciously think about, at least not all the time.

Everything is important when trying to make an impression as a great goalkeeper. Even the way you stand on the field matters. Believe me, having, or not having, a good goalkeeper stance can affect the way you play in goal.

The way a keeper stands is a lot more important to this position than many realize. Let's look at why this is, starting with the "ready" position.

- Hands should be by your sides, at the hip level, with palms facing outward
- Bend your back forward a little. To know if you're in the right position, see if you can feel the upper part of your chest tighten slightly. If you can't feel a slight tension then you are not down far enough.
- Bend your knees to about a 45 degree angle. Your feet should be shoulder width apart. This way you are in the right position to either spread your legs open, if you need to, or close them quickly, say when an opponent tries to play a tricky shot between your legs.
- You should be on your toes. This is a phrase that is so common in soccer that it's almost a cliché. Even so, cliché or not, this is very important. Actually, you don't need to be right on your tiptoe, but on the balls of your feet. This is the front part of your foot, just behind the toes.

OK, so now you know what comprises the professional ready position for a goalkeeper. It's not difficult, though it may take a little practice before you're doing it without any conscious thought.

Let's now look a little closer at the reasons behind this position, starting with the hands.

You have your hands at the sides of your body, at hip level, for a reason. It allows you to extend them and reach out in an instant. This obviously gives you a better chance of stopping fast moving balls.

If your hands are too low, you may have trouble saving high balls on time. Likewise, if your hands are too close to your body, it will take a while longer to fully extend your arms.

In soccer, just one or two seconds delay can make the difference between a goal and a saved shot. So having your hands at your sides, at hip level, means you can extend your arms and hands anywhere, in an instant.

Now let's look at the reason behind your bent back and knees. This stance allows you to jump and dive both quickly and freely. By bending your knees and leaning forward slightly lets you put more power into your jumps.

This means you can stretch your body to its max and reach balls aimed at the highest parts of the goal. This is really useful for those awkward high shots, especially those directed at the two upper corners.

Being able to jump and dive quickly is also why you're on the balls of your feet, as by doing so you get to jump higher. Another advantage of being on the balls of your feet is that you can move away (accelerate) faster. It also enables you to move with more agility.

This is something you will have to do a lot of whenever you play against a team who passes the ball a lot near to the goal area. FC Barcelona is a good example of this style of team attack.

Finally, your feet being shoulder-width apart provides a good base for when you're in the ready position.

Having the feet too close or too wide can leave you in an awkward position, depending on the situation. It can be difficult to move quickly if you don't start with your feet at the right distance apart. And as I pointed out earlier, being able to use your feet effectively in breakaway situations is crucial.

It will determine whether you get to save the breakaway or not, that's how important this is. See, when you're out facing an attacker, the easier and safest play for him is to either place the ball right next to your feet or between your legs.

I have covered all the leg reflexes in a later chapter. When you get to that, make sure you apply everything listed in that section.

OK, it is now up to you to practice the ready position. Keep at it until such a time that you do it naturally, and that means without thinking.

It is so important that you get good at the "ready" position. This is the stance that all professional goalkeepers take when preparing themselves for action.

If you want get as good as you can be, then this has to be your only ready position. It takes longer to write and read about it than it does to actually practice. Just remember to be mindful of all the components as you become familiar with this. To recap, these are hands, shoulders, knees, and feet.

So remember to keep your hands to your sides, and at hip level. Bend your knees and your back slightly. Stay on the balls of your feet and keep them at shoulder width apart.

4. Watch Professional Soccer

I'm going to assume you bought this book because you want to become a great soccer goalkeeper. It is my guess that you are keen to lean all the tricks and maneuvers of the goalkeeping greats. It is the purpose of this book to deliver on all aspects of this #1 position.

It's important that you know the one thing that all successful keepers are consistent about. That is… they ALL spend hours watching and studying professional soccer. This is something that you will want to start doing too.

There is a difference between watching a game and studying the footage. The former is for enjoyment whereas the latter is for educational purposes. It's important not to get these two mixed up.

We are lucky these days as we have YouTube and other media options from where to get free video. It wasn't always like this, not even a generation ago.

Anyway, you have this available to you today, so please make sure you use it. Being able to study those who have gone before you is an opportunity you should definitely not pass up.

In order to be the best, you have to learn from the best. It's as simple as that really. This is why watching the pros in your own time, and at your own pace, is an important step in you becoming a great goalkeeper.

Spend some quality time watching the best keepers, both past and present. Study those who are currently playing like Manuel Neuer, Gianluigi Buffon, David De Gea, Petr Cech and Iker Casillas.

For the goalies that have stopped playing consider Peter Schmeichel, Edwin van der Sar, David Seaman, Oliver Kahn, and any others you might want to add to the list.

Watch videos and live games of pro goalkeepers in action. Pay particular attention to Schmeichel and Van der Sar. These two are the best of the best at the time of writing. You will soon have a good insight into their mentality and their goalkeeping styles. Watch them carefully and take notes.

Before too long you will get to pick up on why they are so good at what they do. Just as important is that you will also spot why lesser keepers are struggling.

This will include you too, to some extent.

Couple this footage with these "44 Steps for Great Soccer Goalie Skills" and you have the best tools ever at your disposal. It's important to note that knowledge alone is useless. You need to act on your newfound information if you're to excel as a goalie. I'm sure you will, but I had to mention this all the same ;)

Time for Action…

Once you have plenty of ideas that you want to try, get to work and see if you can perform some of the moves of the great goalkeepers. If you can apply a few of the things they do into your game, you will eventually develop your own unique style. This way you get to find out what works for you.

You will also discover what doesn't work, and that's equally as important. Feel free to improvise on anything you want. You certainly don't want to try and become a carbon copy of someone you idolize. Yes, we all know the rules, and yes we all know the moves. But it is our own unique twist on things that sets us apart as individuals.

You will never learn the best strategies for goalkeeping until you expose yourself to all the different styles out there. This is why it's so important to study as much as you can from the goalkeeping greats.

This way you get to take what you want and leave behind what you don't. Working like this is by far the best way to develop your game. The more styles you have to work with, the more options you have for shaping your own goalkeeping skills.

So what is it exactly that you get from studying these videos? Well, to begin with you can identify when it's safe to come outside of the box in one-to-one situations when there is a through ball.

You will also get to see whether you should come out to clear the ball with your feet or stay and wait for the attacker to come to you. Study when and why the great keepers make the decisions they do. I can promise that you will get to identify certain patterns over time.

Develop Your Own Style

Don't forget that some moves will work for one keeper but not another. The reasons for this vary. For example, not all keepers have the same build, strength, speed and character. How they perform as individuals depends on these things.

There will also be other maneuvers and ways of playing that all keepers do follow. What you do, and the way you play, will come down to your own individual characteristics.

It will also depend on how much you learn, along with your commitment to improve. All these things will play a role in how you turn out as a goalkeeper.

Dealing with Crosses

Pay particular attention on how to deal with crosses. Also learn when best to stay and when to leave your goal area whenever the ball is near the penalty area.

All situations are unique, that much is true. However, you will still get to identify what decisions are best suited to you personally, at the various stages of your development.

Study other keepers and develop your own game based on what you pick up and practice. Embrace mistakes and make sure you learn from them. These are the golden rules that you need to adhere to. These are the very things that will help shape you quicker than you would ever have thought possible.

Preparing for the Attack

Another important thing for you to study is where to position yourself when the opposing team is on the attack. See how the professionals cut off the angles and deal with aggressive attacks.

Try to replicate their style in your next game or practice. Remember to tweak and develop things to suit who you are and the way you play. The more you get to learn about yourself, both good and bad, the faster you will develop.

Learn How to Punt

You also need to know how to punt pro-style. As you watch the professionals at work, you will see how their long, accurate punts can change the course of a game with a single kick.

This is a skill that many lesser goalies fail to develop. If you become good at getting rid of the ball with strong accurate punts, you will develop an undeniable edge over those who are not so good.

As a goalkeeper, you are not only the last line of defense but also the first line of attack. It's important that you know how to execute a counterattack and how to distribute the ball wisely.

Once you get good at these skills you can create threatening passes. These are all things that you can learn from studying professional goalkeepers. Studying, as opposed to just watching, lets you see the game in a completely different light.

Most of what you learn from watching footage of the world's greatest goalies will also be covered in this book.

Read about what you watch, and watch what you read about. This is the perfect way to reinforce your learning. It is what gives you those "aha" moments, and helps to make perfect sense of everything.

Learn from the Mistakes of Others

We learn more from mistakes than we could ever from successes. Every single professional goalkeeper will tell you this. As a young ambitious goalie, you must view mistakes and common blunders as your friend.

Never ever put yourself down in front of others or beat yourself up when you fail to do something. Look at it as a great opportunity to see what it was that you did wrong, and then work toward correcting it.

Even professional goalies make mistakes. You need to identify their errors, or weak points, as much as their skills and strengths.

That's right, you can also learn from the mistakes of others as well as your own. Knowing what NOT to do is just as important as knowing what to do in any given situation.

When you view goals that professional keepers concede, try to pinpoint how they happened. By that, I mean try to figure out whether the keeper could've done better.

What other action or actions could he have made to save the day? Imagine if it were you in the same situation. How would you have made the save, if possible, now that you have identified how the ball got through?

Not all goalie mistakes result in lost goals. Soccer is a fast-moving game where sometimes even a blunder can result in your favor. It all depends on how the surrounding chaos pans out. Still, it's obviously better not to make mistakes whenever possible.

But there will be times when things move just too fast, and get too chaotic, that mistakes become inevitable. Hindsight is a wonderful thing, but make sure you use it to learn from, and not as something to beat yourself up with.

Who's Doing What?

As a goalie yourself, studying professional keepers is obviously important for your own growth, but it doesn't stop there. For your development, it is also important to gain an insight into the other positions on the field as well.

There's so much more to being a great goalkeeper than just waiting for the ball to come your way. Why? It's because there's usually a lot to learn in the lead up to any attack.

Keeping a close eye on the game as a whole puts you in a better position when the time comes for you to spring into action.

By studying professional defenders, you get to learn what they do to beat their opponents. Furthermore, you also get to see what areas of the field to direct your own defenders to. Studying professional soccer gives you an insight into your enemies (the other team's attackers).

When studying, as opposed to watching for pleasure, you get to see what makes the forwards tick. Understanding the game out on the field will make you more effective at stopping attacks at your own goal.

Reading the game is something that all the great goalkeepers can do. It allows them to better position themselves in any given situation. They are also better able to communicate with their teammates.

Reading the game makes a goalkeeper more effective at everything he does. The better he gets at reading the game, the more successful he is at defeating his opponents.

Reading the game is a skill that you will definitely want to develop as best you can. It doesn't matter if you're fast on your feet or can jump real high. Even if you have incredible reflexes, none of this is of much use if you're unable to read the game.

The best way you can learn to read the game, besides playing it, is by studying professional competitions. Again, note the word "study" here. When you study, as opposed to watch for pleasure, you're engaged in a totally different way.

5. Learn to Catch the Ball Without Injury

The first thing to remember when catching a soccer ball is always get the hands to the ball first. A good goalie uses his arms, back and legs to cushion the ball. This is especially important with powerful shots.

It might sound simple enough, but there is actually a right way and a wrong way to catch a soccer ball. If you don't catch it right, you risk injuring yourself. When catching a soccer ball, your body must always be behind it, though not everybody knows that.

As a goalkeeper you get to use your hands a lot. This means you need to learn to use those hands to best effect. Stopping the ball without hurting yourself is a skill. And like all other skills, this is something that needs mastering to be effective.

As simple as the concept seems, learning to catch a ball properly is not quite as easy as it sounds. This is something which needs proper technique. OK, with that said, let's now look at what this technique involves, and what you can do to improve your catches.

To demonstrate this "proper technique" we will split catching into three different parts. The first is to catch the ball in the air, at chest or face height. I'm talking about high balls here, not corners.

Catching corners is a bit more complicated and requires a separate chapter. For this reason, I've delayed catching corners for now. OK, so the second part is to catch the ball at waist height and just below. And the third is to catch the ball at your knee/foot level, or on the ground.

Once you use the proper technique for catching a soccer ball you will almost never get hurt. So let's now look at just how to do this in a safe and effective manner.

The first thing you need to know about is how to form the proper shape with your hands. The way to catch any ball in the air that's heading towards your face is with the "W" shape, known as the contour catch.

In fact, The "W" catch is the one used for any ball from about waist height up. So as you catch the ball in your hands, your two thumbs should be looking upwards and touching, or almost touching, each other. Do this now to see the "W" shape with your hands.

Besides making the perfect "W" shape with your hands, it's also important to know where to catch the ball. It's always better, whenever possible, to catch the ball at the top. Catching it this way makes it easier to control. Furthermore, if it rebounds you can always bounce it down and simply pick it up again.

Always make sure you face the ball as you catch it. If a ball is coming in at your side, don't just turn to your side and catch that way. Instead, shuffle quickly to the side and catch it head-on, with your body facing completely forward to the ball.

If you turn to catch the ball and mess up, your body won't be behind it. That means it could end up whizzing past you and into the goal. If you're facing the ball directly, it could still hit your body if you fail to catch it with your hands. This way you still get to stop it from entering the goal.

Let's move on now to catching balls at waist height and below. For these catches your hands need to be behind the ball. It's your pinkies (little fingers) this time that should touch or almost touch each other.

As you catch the ball, you need to bend your arms toward your body so that the ball nestles securely against it.

This is called "bagging the ball," where you end up with the ball cradled against your stomach or lower chest area. When caught properly, you shouldn't hurt your stomach or lower chest as your arms will absorb most of the power from the shot.

Finally, let's look at how to deal those low balls. There are several techniques for catching, scooping, or picking up ground or rolling balls.

The first is to simply pick up and bag the ball while standing up straight, or with the knees slightly bent. This is the simplest technique for catching these types of balls.

A word of warning though: only use this method when there are no forwards anywhere near you. Once the ball is at your hands, your pinkies should be touching. From there you just scoop up the ball and bring it into your body.

The next technique for catching balls on the ground is the knee-down pickup. The way to make this catch is to first bend one knee. The other knee goes down almost to the ground, but not quite, and should be very close to the other heel. It's important that the down knee doesn't touch the ground, and nor should it bear any weight.

This way the keeper can get up quick and easy if he needs to. Also, the gap between heel and knee should be less than ball-width. Any wider and there's always the risk of the ball travelling between the legs and into the goal behind. This is something which is really embarrassing for any keeper.

The position looks like you're tebowing (praying on one knee), but don't let that put you off. This kind of save is actually one of the least used because it restricts mobility quite a bit. It's still important to learn this way of catching low balls nonetheless.

It gives the keeper the largest backstop for ground balls, helping to save shots that may otherwise be difficult intercept.

This style of saving a ground-rolling ball is best on long, low, hard shots, on wet grass, or uneven fields. Once the ball gets to your hands, the technique for picking it up is the same as that from the standing position.

The final form of ground catch is the most difficult of all three. To perform this you will have to wait until the ball reaches you before making your move.

Here you need to scoop the ball up and bag it while leaning your body forward. If you do this correct, you will end by lying on the ground with the ball safely tucked away underneath your body.

This is difficult to master, but a commonly used catch nonetheless. The reason for this is because it's a lot safer than the other two in situations where you are dealing with fast or strong shots. It is especially useful for saving fast balls that bounce off the ground and rocket towards you.

So there you have it, the different ways to catch all kinds of different shots. By following these instructions you will be able to get your body behind the ball and catch many more shots fired at your goal. Don't forget too, performing these saves correctly means you avoid unnecessarily hurting yourself in the process.

Worth noting is that even when you use proper techniques, there is always some risk of injury to your hands. This usually occurs with jamming the fingers and finger sprains. These things are likely to happen not by a successful catch but by physical clashes on the field. Sometimes there is nothing you can do to avoid jamming a finger.

That said you can reduce the risk of injury a lot by strengthening the hands and fingers. There are also exercises that will help to increase the range of motions in parts of the hand. Warming up your muscles before playing a game, or practicing, also helps and should be a given.

To avoid finger sprains I recommend you invest in a pair of gloves with finger guards, or finger saves. These are the newest invention for goalie gloves. Their specific purpose is to prevent spraining the fingers.

These are small pieces of metal that insert into every finger of your glove, except for the thumbs. Their main function is to prevent your fingers from hyper-extending backwards. They do a great job at that too.

As for choosing the right gloves, well, it's important that you try before you buy. I would advise against shopping online for gloves with finger guards.

The reason is that some will not allow you to bend your fingers forward far enough. That is something which would obviously make catching the ball quite difficult. This is why you need to try the gloves on before buying.

As or the gloves themselves, make sure you find a style that you feel comfortable wearing. There are three types of glove palms, namely roll finger, flat and negative cut. Each palm has their good and bad points.

What's important is that you get decide which is best for you personally. The only way to do that is to try them on and see how they feel.

OK, that's hands and catches sorted. Next up we look at how to throw like a pro.

6. Become an Expert at Throws

A good goalie is an expert at throws. In soccer, an attack will often start with the keeper. This is certainly the case right after a corner kick or a free kick that the goalkeeper caught.

As a goalkeeper, you are the one who should be able to distribute the ball to any of your teammates to most places on your side of the field. Once you have delivered the ball safely, the field player can start going toward the other goal.

This means you must be able to pass the ball to your teammates accurately. You do this by using either your hands (throws) or your feet (kicks).

There are various types of ball distribution in the game of soccer, e.g. goal kicks, punts, and throws, etc. Whatever the type used, they all fit into one of two categories, "throws" and "kicks." The individual types of distribution have their own place in the game. As for throws, you have two options.

Throws tend to be much shorter than kicks. The keeper will always throw the ball whenever the situation warrants it.

This is because it is a more accurate way to distribute the ball than a kick. The first style is the basic throw. This is where you throw the ball high in the air toward your teammates.

These types of throws are common for counter attacks. This is when the keeper makes the decision to quickly shift the play from the penalty area to the middle of the field.

There are three different types of throws that you send through the air to your teammate. In this chapter we take a look at the benefits of all three throws, along with how to perform each one properly.

The other type of throw is a roll. A roll is the most accurate throw but with the shortest distribution. Rolls are also the easiest way for your teammates to receive the ball. You can send balls along the ground whenever you want to calm the game down for a moment.

Another time is when you realize the opposition has already reorganized on their side of the field. Once that happens, you don't have any chance to create a fast counter attack, hence the roll throw to nearby teammates.

OK, let us start by taking a look at rolls. Rolling the ball out to your teammates is almost the same as rolling a bowling ball. As pointed out previously, rolls are also the easiest and most accurate form of ball distribution.

To do a perfect roll pass, you have to start by holding the ball low to the ground. It's important to control the ball between the palm of the hand and the forearm.

You also need to keep your wrist bent. When you're ready, step with the opposite foot, and "bowl" the ball. As you do this, make sure your fingertips brush the ground.

Note that this move requires you to bend your knees and waist. This way you get low enough to smoothly follow through with the action. Keep in mind that rolling the ball needs performing in one complete motion. When done correctly, the ball goes along the ground at a good pace, arriving safely at your teammate's feet.

Now let's look at high throws. Throwing the ball through the air out to your teammates is one of the best ways to get your side quickly moving in the right direction.

The reason why this is so effective is because it's an excellent way to start counterattacks. When you throw the ball like this you get to clear it away from your goal and closer to the rival goal. It's a great way to get your team into attack mode quickly.

Throwing the ball in the air is also a lot more accurate and a lot safer than punting or kicking generally. This is especially the case when the player you want to send the ball to is not on the side parallel to your dominant foot. This isn't such an issue if you have learned to use both feet effectively (recommended).

So it's extremely important to learn how to throw the ball far and with accuracy. Let's now take a look at how to perform the best throws possible.

First, there is the overhand throw, or sling. In order to do a good overhand throw you have to extend your arm fully to the back, and then fully to the front. Your arm should start low and end up going over your head before releasing the ball.

As you extend your arm forward, you should also step forward with the same foot as the hand you are using to throw the ball. So if you're throwing with your right hand, then you step forward with your right foot.

Point to note: As you do the throw, make sure you don't bend at the elbow. In other words, keep the throwing arm completely straight.

The overhand throw allows you to get the farthest distance of any throw, but it's also the least accurate of them all. This can still be a very effective throw when done well. It is without doubt the most difficult throw, from a technical perspective at least.

This is because the hand must stay on top of the ball throughout the 180 degrees or so arc. This is more difficult than it sounds, especially when you're trying to be accurate at the same time. I suggest you practice this throw so that you can add it to your arsenal of skills and call on it when the need arises.

The next high throw to look at is what goalkeeper coaches call the sidearm throw. This is more accurate than the overhand throw but less accurate than the Javelin or Baseball Throw (next). It's also between the other two in terms of distance and delivery.

The sidearm throw is where your arm extends slightly behind your body. Note that the ball is not completely stationed to the side of your body, despite its name.

It's at a three-quarters angle, just below shoulder level. With the sidearm throw, you send the ball forward in a sweeping motion. The move uses a bit of a sweeping, or slinging motion to send the ball on its way.

OK, let's move on to the final of the high throws. This one is the baseball throw, or javelin, so called because it's performed similar to how you would throw a javelin. It's the most accurate of the three.

To do the baseball throw you have to position the ball in your palm, and to the side of your head. The idea is to then push the ball forward with your hand toward your teammate, just as you step into the throw. If you can create some backspin on the ball that will help. This way the ball will "sit down," making it easier to receive.

Like the sidearm throw, the baseball throw is quite accurate when done properly. It cannot be used to send the ball to wider spaces though, or go as far as the overhead throw.

There are several benefits to high throws and roll passes when sending balls to your teammates. Each situation will determine which throw to use to best effect. Before you have that choice though, you first need to become skilled at the different styles of throw.

To summarize this chapter:

Make sure you learn how to do roll passes. These are excellent for playing the ball to your teammates nearby. They are also the most accurate of all the throws.

Also, find out what type of air throw works best for you. Some keepers will prefer the sidearm whereas others might like the overhead. Then again, someone else will choose the baseball throw more often than not. It all depends in the individual. It's important that you master each of these, even though you will likely use one style above all the others.

Once you get to practice them all, you will soon find out which one you feel most comfortable with. The one you throw the farthest, and with the most accuracy, might actually surprise you.

Despite your preferences, make sure you master all the throwing skills. A great goalkeeper should be able to do anything and everything on the field that's required of him, as situations arise. The more you can do the more options you have.

And the more options open to you, the better you become. Use whatever you can to do your job to best effect. Learn everything there is to know about accurate throws. Get good at throwing and you will be yet another step closer to becoming a great all-round goalie.

Remember, if you need encouragement, inspiration, and new ideas, don't forget to study the goalkeeping greats on video. In fact, do this anyway. Try to make studying videos a good habit whenever you're learning something new. Watch plenty of professional games on the TV as well.

Go to live, professional games if you get the opportunity. Whatever skill you're working on at the time is the skill you need to zoom in on and take notes of. Also pay attention to how many goals come about as a direct or indirect result of goalkeepers starting an attack.

I definitely recommend you watch footage of the German goalkeeper, Manuel Neuer. He's the goalkeeping superstar who plays for the German side, Bayern Munich FC. Watch to see how much he participates in many of his team`s successful wins. If you haven't studied him up close yet, then you're in for a real treat.

7. Be Intimidating

They say that attacking players should be scared of the keeper, and they're right, they should. When goalies are intimidating, most attacking players do not want to get into one-to-one situations with them. That's great news for both the keeper and his team as it means the attacking player won't be on his best form.

Being big and strong will make any goalkeeper look and feel a bit intimidating. But physical size alone won't cut it. In fact, many goalies do not have that kind of physique anyway. Being able to catch balls, dive well, and intercept shots is all well and good.

But skills and bravery won't make you intimidating either, at least not by themselves. For a keeper to come across as intimidating to his opponents he needs to master something else.

That something else is his psychological game. That's right; how you play your mental game can be just as important as the physical one. Mind games, for want of a better expression, can make or break any play.

Being able to engage and win mental battles with opposing forwards is an advantage for any goalie. In fact, it will take your game up to a whole new level. No matter how skillful your opponents happen to be, you have the opportunity to disrupt them.

If they find themselves mentally intimidated by your presence, then you're onto a winner. When a player feels intimidated he plays less well than when he is not. It's as simple as that. This is why having an intimidating stance can work in your favor.

This is a skill just like any other. That means you can develop it with the right training. So you might be wondering how to train yourself to be mentally intimidating. What if it's not your nature?

What if you're easy going, how can you learn to throw feelings of doubt and fear into the mind of your opponents? Well, it's not as difficult as it might seem. You can learn how to act in a certain way when you play soccer that is totally alien to your usual character. Let's look at how you might do this.

The Voice

The first thing you need to work on is how to use your voice to best effect. The sounds and words which come out of your mouth matter when playing the mental game. Words and sounds are what most goalies use to intimidate their opponents.

Note that there is nothing in this which breaks the rules. This is not verbal abuse we're talking about here. Yelling or insulting opponents shows a loss of control.

Losing control is not how you intimidate rival players. Not only will it lose you respect, but you will become a laughing stock. And if the ref catches you being abusive, there's the risk of getting a colored card for unsportsmanlike behavior.

Furthermore, intimidating in a bulling manner will more than likely have a reverse affect. It will put you out of focus and the opponent will be more determined than ever to play well. So now you know the wrong way, let's now get back to the right way to intimidate opponents using the voice.

The secret is to be loud. That's all there is to it. Don't be afraid to make as much noise as you like whenever you're going for the ball. This includes words and sounds. Think it's too simple? That's because it is, but don't let simplicity fool you.

I can promise you this has an effect, and a good one at that, on any player you're playing against. The only thing you need to do is be convincing. This is what I was talking about when I spoke of acting. If you're not loud by nature, then you have to learn to act like the wild man when you're playing in goal.

Shout "KEEPER!" at the top of your lungs. Make it so loud that they can hear you on the other side of the field. Remember to wear your wild man's expression as you do this. Having a big smile taking up two thirds of your face as you call out won't have quite the same effect.

If you look and sound convincing, your opponents will be put off and more cautious. That means they won't be as confident when challenging you for a ball in the air or on the ground. Even slight caution brings with it some hesitation. A little hesitancy is exactly the result you're looking for here.

OK, so you have your voice sorted out now, or you will have once you get to work on it. Any other talents you have will further reinforce your intimidation tactics.

So skill, bravery to challenge and plenty of noise is going to make you a force to be reckoned with. Any player who enters your domain will not relish the challenge he is about to encounter.

You want forwards to question whether they ought to go in with a tackle against you. You want them to look for easier, softer ways around you as this will pose less of a threat. You want them to think in the back of their minds how you will take anyone out who DARES to challenge you.

Okay, so your bark might be a lot worse than your bite, but they don't need to know that. All you need to do is intimidate them and see how things play out. If you're convincing, you are going to be very happy at how well your new approach works.

A strong voice is also useful for when challenging opponents for high balls that are yet to land. Here you have to use your voice to show the other team that YOU are going up in the air and WILL WIN that ball no matter what.

They have to realize that they are in your domain now, as unwanted visitors as it were. Get this right and your opponents will want to get in and out of your space as quick as possible. In other words, they feel pressured to rush, and that's a good thing.

I can remember when I used to play soccer as a kid, on the local green near my home. Every once in a while the ball would go over a fence and into the garden of this grumpy man. He would get so annoyed with us whenever this happened. He never did anything more than raise his voice and give us a good telling off.

Still, his ranting and bulging eyes would put the fear of god into us nonetheless. We all feared knocking on his door to ask if we could please have our ball back.

We used to toss a coin for it, that's how big a deal it was. Sometimes, one of us would sneak over his fence, hoping he wouldn't see us. Other times we would have to knock his door. It all depended where the ball ended landed. So why am I telling you all of this?

Well, your domain on the soccer field is your back garden now. You are the grumpy guy that everyone fears. The opposing defenders are the kids who have just kicked the ball into your yard. Their job is to try to get to it before you get to them, but it's not something they relish.

Grow Bigger

Another way to intimidate your opponents is to make yourself appear physically bigger. I already covered the way you should stand in chapter three. There we looked at ways to develop the right goalkeeper stance. But let's now look at why your stance will not only help you save the ball, but also help to intimidate your opponents.

As the rivals approach, you have to change your body language. The way to do this is by having your hands out to the sides, chest puffed up, and feet shoulder width apart.

These are small changes that can play a big role in your favor. By standing this way you are spreading yourself out more. You suddenly become a much bigger presence inside the goal area. It's an illusion, of course, but it's one that works when done well.

Being unpredictably loud and altering your stance is all about the mental battle. You are, in fact, playing mind games. Sometimes, you have to challenge your opponents at the subconscious level. Winning takes what it takes.

It means using anything that works in your favor without breaking the rules. Becoming intimidating is just one more tactic in your skills arsenal that you should exploit to your full advantage.

Some time ago I was watching the Community Shield game in England between Arsenal and Chelsea. In case you're not familiar, the Community Shield is the game played in England before the beginning of each new season.

It's between the Premier League`s champion (in this case Chelsea) and the FA Cup champions (Arsenal). The Community Shield in England is like the Super Cup played in the other European countries.

Anyway, as I was enjoying the game with friends, I noticed just how intimidating Chelsea's goal keeper was. His name is Thibaut Courtois. Honestly, this guy made me nervous just watching him.

As an Arsenal fan, I always like to see my team scoring as many goals as possible. It's even more rewarding when they beat a tough rival like Chelsea.

In this particular game, Arsenal was dominating.

Even so, those of us watching were beginning to think that Keeper Courtois was unbeatable. The way the Chelsea goalie handled situations was awe-inspiring. We wished he wasn't so good, but you couldn't help but admire the man's style.

The way he dealt with one-to-one situations and attacks near the penalty area was impressive to say the least. I'm not exaggerating here. Every single ball played inside Chelsea's penalty area was nerve-racking.

Courtois would come out of his goal like a man possessed. He would spread himself in an intimidating way, like some kind of superhero out of a Marvel comic book.

It's sad to say, but all the Arsenal attacking players looked hopeless and helpless whenever they faced Courtois. This was especially the case with close-range balls. You could see the Arsenal players shift their style; they had no choice.

They did this in their desperate attempts to defeat the keeper. They had to shoot wide instead of playing their usual, more controlled passing style.

The only goal Arsenal scored that day was from a strong ball shot from outside the penalty area. This was a great goal, and an impressive kick, but it was still a desperate attempt nonetheless. Why the desperation? Well, to put it simply, the Chelsea keeper intimidated the Arsenal players.

They were afraid of the way Courtois came out of his goal and challenged them every single time. In other words, they had lost confidence in their ability to score against him in his own domain. He had got to them all, and that's the point.

This is how you should be when playing against your opponents, especially the skilled ones. You need to be brave, and you should act as though you fear no one.

Even if it's not how you feel on the inside, you must give the right impression on the outside. Control your stance and look menacing. Be brave and challenge them all.

Make plenty of noise and put the fear of god into anyone who DARES to enter your domain. It's time to build your reputation so that you become known as the "Goalkeeper from Hell."

8. Learn How to Save Penalty Kicks

Goalkeepers often fear penalty kicks as much as the player does taking them. It's important to be calm in these situations though. How you appear to the penalty taker can play a big part in how he performs.

This is another of those times where the mental game comes into play. The pressure is on the shooter who's taking the penalty, so use that to your advantage. The cooler you are in these situations, the more agitated the penalty taker becomes. Everyone expects the penalty taker to score. No one expects the goalkeeper to save.

The outcome of a penalty kick can often be unpredictable though, and surprise everyone. There are always expectations, but never any guaranteed results. This is why there is so much pressure on when teams prepare for penalties.

Playing in goal doesn't get any easier in modern football, that's for sure. But then no keeper would want it to. After all, the challenge is where the fun is. Even so, notice how soccer balls are getting too light and too fast these days. This makes it easier for attackers and midfielders to score from greater distances. It also makes it harder for the keeper to save these modern balls.

The mere essence of soccer is to score more goals, not save more shots or penalty kicks. Goalkeeper's have their own excuses when they fail to save penalties. Some might be justified, others will be lame. However, the blame game does not serve anyone well.

Remember how we looked at learning from mistakes and blunders earlier, so that we can improve our game. Well, finding excuses is not what you might call a learning experience, it's a punishing one.

Whenever you beat yourself up for failing to save a shot, penalty or otherwise, you are tearing down your potential, as opposed to building it up. It's never easy to save penalty shots. That doesn't mean it's impossible though, because it's not. Goalkeepers save penalties all the time. Others shots go completely wide of the goal, such is the pressure on the penalty taker.

There are a few things you can do to save or prevent penalties from succeeding. Below are some tips for you to consider whenever you`re trying to save or deflect a penalty kick:

- *Don't just try to guess.* This is the strategy that below average keepers use when trying to save penalty kicks. It's a shot in the dark approach that rarely pays off. So as the shooter is deciding what side to send the ball, you shouldn't just pick a side and hope for the best. You have to learn how to read the penalty taker's intentions (see below). Sometimes he will be good at hiding his intent, but you have to try. It's certainly better than guessing.

- *Watch the shooter's eyes.* Observing the eyes can give you some kind of sign of which direction he is likely to send the ball. Can you see him look toward a certain side? If he is, he may intend to shoot to that side. On the other hand, he might be trying to trick you and end up going the other way. While this in itself involves some guessing, it is still better than guessing blind. The best time to watch his eyes is early on, before he stands on the penalty spot to place the ball. This is the most sincere and honest look the striker will make during a penalty. Your job as the keeper is to try and figure out what the penalty taker is about to do. Note that there will usually be a lot of bluffing involved in this process. Whichever direction he looks in just before taking the shot, is most likely to be a bluff. So the look you want to focus on the most is where his eyes fleetingly glance before he even touches the ball.

- *Watch the shooter's plant foot.* The plant foot is the opposite of the foot he uses to strike the ball. So if the shooter kicks the ball with his right foot, then the plant foot is the left one, and vice versa. So how can watching the shooter's plant foot be an advantage to you for saving the penalty? The secret is in the direction it points to. If the plant foot is pointing to your right side, the ball is more likely to be going that way. Likewise, if the plant foot points to your left side, there is a high possibility that penalty taker will shoot the ball toward your left.
- *Watch the shooter's hips.* This is a bit like watching his plant foot. As the shooter takes the kick, see how his hips open up and point in certain way. Just as the ball is likely to go in the direction of the shooter's plant foot, it is also likely to go in the same direction as his hips suggest.

- *Don't dive too soon.* This is about as much use as guessing. Penalty takers often wait for the keeper to make a move before they even strike the ball. This is even more likely now that referees allow shooters to almost stop completely in their run up to the ball. You will see some penalty takers these days stop completely. If this happens, and you dive too soon, it makes the job of the one taking the penalty so much easier. Imagine that. You could be diving to the right, for example, and the striker hasn't even touched the ball. How to do it right… Just wait until the penalty taker touches the ball. If he was intending to pause briefly, then he won't catch you out if you wait. It's all about split second timing. Try to read his intentions and wait right up until the moment of impact before making your dive. This will put you in a much better position to save the shot. Note that many players will also kind of jerk a bit, just before hitting the ball. This brief break in their flow is yet another attempt to trick you. Once you get to know all their little tricks you become better at reading their intent. There are no guarantees, but you can still improve your chances all the same.

- Don't dive without catching the ball. What do I mean by that? Well, say you have guessed the correct direction of the ball and are just about ready to save it. Then, right at that moment something awful happens. Either the ball goes under you, or you dive too far and don't even get to touch it. This is what can happen when you're too keen. So when you're facing a penalty kick, don't just jump up and dive a certain way. Instead, side shuffle to the area where you think the penalty taker is going to shoot. This helps you because it doesn't matter if the penalty shooter strikes a high or a low ball. With this approach you'll be able to go either way (high or low). This is not the case if you just decide to dive one way.
- Intimidate the shooter (without breaking any rules). Yelling at the penalty taker will almost guarantee you a yellow card, so don't be tempted to do that. There are legal ways to make the shooter nervous, as we looked at earlier.

To recap:

Be mindful of your stance. Have your arms out. This not only covers more goal area but it also makes you look bigger and more intimidating in the eyes of the penalty taker. Remember to bend your knees too. Bent knees help you to jump better when you dive.

They also add to the intimidation factor. This is because it looks like you're ready to spring into action at any moment, which you are of course.

The way you stand and the way you look plays a central role in the intimidation game. Illusion is all-important in the game of soccer. Don't just take my word for it. There have been various studies into this. Scientists have done research on illusion and looked at how it applies to soccer.

They found that a goalkeeper who has his arms up "appears" bigger. Bigger that is, than if his arms were down by his sides or parallel. He's not bigger, of course. But he appears to be bigger, and more intimidating, when he positions his arms in a certain way.

You may have heard of the Müller-Lyer Illusion, which is one of the most famous of all illusions. In this experiment, two lines appear to be of different lengths even though they are exactly the same.

You can look at the lines for as long as you want to, but one will always appear longer than the other. It's the same principle when a goalkeeper places his arms out. Of course he hasn't gotten bigger, but he appears to have, and that's why it works.

The position of your arms is not the only way to mess with the shooters head as you prepare to save the penalty. There are other clever "body tricks" you can use which also cause distraction.

To illustrate this point we can use a real-word example. Let's take a look at how Liverpool won the 2005 UEFA Champions league against AC Milan. We join the game at the back end, where there was a penalty shootout.

Liverpool was three goals behind and yet managed to tie the score by the final whistle. The coaches called this comeback "The Istanbul Miracle." Liverpool F.C. had one of the best European goalkeepers at the time, well known for saving penalties. This was the Polish keeper Jerzy Dudek.

Dudek played for Liverpool between 2001 and 2007, before leaving to Real Madrid. What he did during that 2005 UEFA Champions league was perhaps the game of his life. Liverpool fans still chant his name to this day. This gives you some idea of how treasured he became for his performance on that special day.

Not everyone reading here will know what went down on that famous 2005 penalty shootout against Milan, so here it is, in brief. Jerzy Dudek "DANCED" in goal. I'm not kidding. Dudek kept flipping, dancing, jumping and moving backward and forward, first to the right, then to the left.

He moved all over the place as the Italians tried to prepare for their penalties. Was it intimidating; did this act as a distraction? You bet it did. By dancing all over the place Dudek also made his goal look smaller to the Italians. They missed three out of their five penalties.

To realize how great Dudek was you have to know who two of the three players were who missed their penalties. One was AC Milan's Andrea Pirlo, and the other Andrey Shevechenko. These guys were penalty experts and they shouldn't have missed, but they did. The third missed penalty was by the Brazilian Sérgio Cláudio dos Santos. Because of Dudek antics, this poor guy couldn`t find anywhere to place his ball, so it ended up outside the goal.

As you can see from this real-world example, all these things I talk of are effective tactics. Moving side to side, across the goal, makes you look bigger and your goal appear smaller. It also helps to take away the shooter's focus, which is always a good thing.

Talking to the penalty shooter (not yelling), can also influence their decision. For example, you can tease the penalty taker by telling him which way you're going to dive. Not that he will take much notice of the details of your chatter, but that's not the point. It's the "legal" distraction that really matters.

In the 2014 Brazil World Cup, the Holland and Newcastle's goalkeeper, Tim Krul, did something quite unusual. He went over to every single Costa Rican player who was taking a penalty against him. He told them that he knew where they would aim their shots. He also got in some other little mind games that he likes to play against his opponents.

This was yet another successful tactic and Krul managed to help his team reach the semifinal. Unfortunately, his team lost against Argentina. It was another competition that went to a penalty shootout.

In this game, the Dutch manager, Louis van Gaal, forgot to save his third substitution for extra time. It meant that he was unable to replace his first keeper, Jasper Cillessen, with the penalty expert Tim Krul.

So you can see how penalty kicks have a lot to do with the mental side of the game. Put lots of focus into this side of things and develop your own unique psychological skills. Get good at messing with the heads of those taking penalties against you. Develop your mental game along with your physical skills. Do these things and watch how you excel as a great goalie.

9. Become an Expert at Punting

It's crucial that you become an expert on punting. Goalkeepers already have the most unique position in soccer as they are the only ones who can legally use their hands.

The keeper's unique position is even better because they get to punt the ball. Punting is the goalkeeper's main way to distribute the ball over a long distance.

No other player on the field gets to drop the ball with their hands and then kick it on the way down. It's a skill that comes in very useful at times, and one that you need to master as soon as you can.

Besides being unique, punting is also an important part of goalkeeping. It is often the best way to distribute the ball fast, with accuracy, and over a good distance.

Like other types of distribution, such as throws, there are various kinds of punting. Let's take a closer look at each of them, along with how to perform them correctly. There are three in total, all having their own benefits.

The Punt

The basic punt is pretty straightforward. To perform it accurately you drop the ball straight down a moment before you start to bring your kicking leg up. The idea is to volley the ball downfield with the leg opposite to the hand from which you dropped the ball.

To do the volley itself, pull your kicking leg far back, then extend through (with your leg and ankle locked), and hit the ball. Remember to drop the ball down and not toss it up in the air.

The benefit of punts is that they are great for distance and height. The downside of the basic punt is that it's the least accurate type of punting.

Punts are especially useful when your team has been under pressure for a while. You can add some much needed relief to the game by punting the ball downfield.

The Drop Kick

This, in my opinion, is the hardest type of punt to do well. It is also the most uncommon of all three punts. But drop kicks can also be very helpful when done correctly. To do a drop kick, you use pretty much the same technique as punting.

The main difference with the dropkick is with the actual ball drop. Instead of kicking the ball out of the air and sending it downfield, you drop it to the ground first. When the ball bounces back up you strike it.

Dropkicks are useful because they are the most accurate form of punting. But accuracy only comes after you have mastered the skill, of course. They can be a little tricky to get right at first. So the sooner you start developing your dropkick skills, the better.

The Sidewinder

The sidewinder is the best form of punting. This is because you can kick the ball over a great distance. This punt also allows you to kick the ball with a lot of power and accuracy.

Both the basic punt and the dropkick require a straight-on volley. The sidewinder does not. As the name implies, this kick requires that you to do a side volley. To do this properly, the ball should be in the opposite hand of your kicking foot. You then need to turn your body slightly to one side. This is your start position.

When you drop the ball it must be at hip level when you send it downfield.

Note: Always drop the ball, whatever type of punt you do, never toss it up.

The sidewinder is a great way to punt. It is also accurate. In fact, it's almost as accurate as a throw. The difference, however, is that you can send the ball much further using a sidewinder than you ever could with a throw.

The sidewinder also sends the ball away at high speed. This extra speed is important when you're trying to start a quick counterattack.

OK, so those are the three main types of punts used by goalkeepers. The sidewinder is quickly becoming the most common of all three. This is for no other reason than it's the most effective.

There will still be situations where it's better to use one of the other two punts. For that reason, it won't hurt to learn how to do them all. If these are all new to you, then I suggest you start learning from the easiest to the hardest. This order is the basic punt first, then sidewinders, and then drop kicks.

Also, by practicing all three of them you get to see which one works the best for you. Just because the majority of keepers use sidewinders, that doesn't necessarily mean you have to use them too.

You might find that you're particularly good at dropkicks, for example, and prefer to use those more so than other types. Just make sure you can perform all three well, and one of them exceptionally well.

It can take a lot of practice to get good at punting, so be patient and persistent in your efforts so that you get to perfect your techniques.

10. Learn How to Deal with Back Passes

This is a fairly common mistake that a lot of keepers make when they receive easy passes from teammates. It's very important for a goalie to know exactly how to deal with back passes. Any keeper who looks surprised when a ball comes back to him from one of his field players has not been reading the game well.

He has, in fact, taken his eyes off the ball, if you'll forgive pun. Always expect the unexpected in soccer. That's the golden rule. And if you're not comfortable with back passes, now is the time to get comfortable.

As you know, good ball distribution is an important part of good goalkeeping. That means it should come as no surprise to you if your teammates feel the need to pass the ball back to you at different times.

Good communication is essential in soccer. It allows a team to operate like a well-oiled unit. Without good communication you don't have a team.

What you do have is a bunch of individuals running around a field kicking a bag of wind about. So whenever a teammate passes the ball back to you, the goalie, he has done so for a reason. If you're working well as a team, you will know why the ball is back over to you, and the game will continue to flow.

Your position also requires that you organize players and delegate jobs to your defense. You can only do this when you are switched on and aware of everything that's going on around you.

Let's set up a situation and then look at how to deal with it. So let's say you have just passed the ball to a teammate and he passes it back to you. Now what?

We'll start at the very beginning, before the ball is even near you. Let's first look at what you shouldn't be doing when one of your defenders has the ball and you're anticipating a back pass. Have you guessed it yet?

That's right, you must move away from the goal mouth. You never want to be standing right in front of the goal when someone passes the ball back to you. We've all seen it before, those embarrassing home goals. Don't, whatever you do, tempt fate.

Even if you're standing away from the front of the goal, a missed pass could still result in a corner kick. Neither of these are situations you want to find yourself in, although one is certainly a lot worse than the other.

OK, let's say that your defender has successfully passed the ball back to you. Your job is to then know exactly what your next move will be.

Whatever it is, it will usually result in you getting rid of the ball as quick as possible. Not only does a keeper have to be quick thinking, but he also needs to be a couple of steps ahead of the game at any given time.

One or two touches should be the most you take when receiving a back pass. This rule is even more important when you're under extreme pressure to push on with the game. Granted, there will be occasions, sometimes, where your team is prepared to give you some time with the ball.

When that happens, you can take as many touches as you want. The important thing is that you're all working in harmony. Everyone has to be on the same page. In other words, you are playing as a team.

Yes you need to be in the "moment." But you also have to be thinking ahead. I know it's a fine balancing act, but as you improve these things will come naturally to you. Hesitation and indecision in these situations will only hurt your prospects.

Another situation where you may need more than two touches is if the rival forward is right on top of you. When this happens, it's not always easy to clear the ball when the opponents are too close.

To start with, there's always the risk of hitting them with the ball as you try to pass it on. It's also easier for an opponent to intercept the ball when they're close by. In these cases you may need to make a few touches on the ball to clear the way for a safer pass.

A good goalkeeper knows how to feint. This comes in handy when you need to fake your intention after a back pass. In this case you make the opponent think you're just about to clear the ball in a certain direction, but you don't. Instead, at the last moment, you touch it to the other side and send it on its way.

When it comes to back passes, always assume the opposition forwards are going to pressure you. That's if they're around, of course. This means you need to get rid of the ball fast, and with as few touches as safely possible.

Master Your Touches

As you know, the opposition forwards are always hungry for the ball. They look for ways to steal it away from you at every opportunity. If your first touch moves the ball too far, you then increase the chance of losing it to the nearby forwards.

It's always best to move the ball along with as few touches as possible. It's equally as important to control those touches and not let them run astray.

You need to make a good impression with your first touch on the ball. If this is something that needs work, I suggest you make it one of your priorities. Develop your first touch so that you can enhance your reaction time.

Controlling the soccer ball on the first touch allows you to make that next pass right away. The less hesitation or fumbling there is, the quicker your team can move on with their game. Not all situations need you to make a pass right away though, but the majority will.

Let's now look closer at what to do when it's time to send the ball back to your teammates after receiving a back pass. Oftentimes, the coach will instruct you to switch the point of attack. This means if you got the ball on the left side he'll want you to now play it toward the right side.

This is where it becomes important that you can play the ball with either of your feet. It's not enough that you can just kick the ball with your weaker foot, but also pass with accuracy over a distance. You must also be able to do this with your non-prominent foot in either one or two touches.

There will be times when you just have to clear the ball far away straight after receiving a back pass. A typical scenario would be when an aggressive forward is right on top of you. Every situation is different, of course. If you've been reading the game well, you will know what moves to make, at least most of the time you will.

Any keeper who is not good at controlling and kicking the ball needs to let his teammates know about it. Allowing the other players send back passes that you can't handle is just asking for trouble. That doesn't mean the goalie can dictate how every move plays out, obviously.

There will always be occasions when a player has to send a back pass to the keeper. But if nothing else, everyone should understand how to deal with various situations before a game starts. For example, it should be clear how to pass the ball back to the keeper with regards to his strength or speed, both inside and outside the penalty area.

Not every goalkeeper can be good at all skills, but if he wants to excel he must be versatile. Only unambitious amateurs accept too many shortcomings in their game. This is why great goalies are masters at receiving back passes and moving the ball on with one touch.

Besides this, all good keepers know how to "scoop" the ball, along with other ball handling skills. You need to look at your game and see if you can identify any areas that could use some improvement. Note anything down that you think needs working on and get practicing without hesitation.

Goalkeepers not only have to save the ball. There are plenty of other situations where they also need to save the day. Sometimes, the keeper has to get more involved in the game near to his goal area.

If your ball receiving and passing skills are not up to par, then it's time to act. I urge you to get working on this area of your game ASAP.

On that note, let's look at a couple of drills that will help you to develop your one-touch skills.

Most first-touch soccer drills are simple. They're all effective too, but they do require lots of training and repetition, and I do mean a lot. The good news is that these drills are quite good fun, so that always helps.

The Wall Drill

The "Wall Drill" is one that you can do at any time and in any place. All you have to do is grab a ball and stand in front of a good solid wall (no windows please!). The idea is to just hit the ball off the wall and then focus on receiving while maintaining good control. Once you get confident with the basics, try to then vary the height and velocity of the passes. You might also want to try using different body parts to control the ball.

Juggling the Ball

Another good way to help develop your first touch skill is to juggle the ball. Juggling is a simple and fun drill. It also works on touch, balance and agility as well, so it's a bonus exercise in that respect.

This is how the exercise goes, starting at a basic level:

Juggle the ball twice on one foot at the laces. You then alternate to the other foot and keep going like this, first with one foot, then the other. It's important not to let the ball bounce.

If it does, don't give up. Just pick up again from where you left off. If you can, try not to let the foot touching the ball touch the ground between touches. Do as many as you can, as often as you can, and you will definitely improve your first touch.

There are plenty of other fun drills for developing this important skill too, so feel free to try them out. The two outlined above should be enough to get you started though.

11. Make Quick Decisions

If a player wastes four opportunities but scores on the fifth, fans will likely chant his name in celebration. If a goalkeeper saves four cracking shots at his goal, yet makes a mistake which lets the fifth one in, he's unsuccessful in the eyes of many fans.

Some may even demand his head on a plate. It will all depend on the current score and in what manner he lost the goal.

This illustrates to you how big the responsibility is that a keeper has to shoulder. It also shows how delicate and important his role is.

The spotlight is always on the goalie when the game moves into his domain. He might be part of the team, but his job can become lonely and pressured when it's time for him to save the day.

Quick wit and fast decision making are the traits of a great goalkeeper. The percentage of good decisions he makes must be high in term of effectiveness and timing.

Furthermore, he must be consistent in this. It's a wonderful feeling when you play the game of your life and end up as the hero who saved the day.

However, you are not as good as a single game. You greatness is measured on your ability to perform consistently well. Effectiveness...?

Any decision a keeper makes should follow one of these three degrees of effectiveness, according to their importance.

- **Degree 1**: Saving the ball completely without creating any new dangers. This means not sending the ball back to the other team once it's saved. For example, when a goalkeeper jumps or goes out of his goal to catch a cross, the highest degree of effectiveness is to catch the ball completely. This also applies when making a dive for a ball. Again, the highest degree of effectiveness for the keeper is to either catch the ball or deflect it in the direction of his nearest defender. Clearing the ball away toward an attacker from the opposite team is the reverse of this. This situation would make it easy for the opponent to shoot the ball back toward the goal.

- **Degree 2**: Saving the ball but the threat is still there. In this situation, the goalkeeper cares only about the save at hand. Many times this will be acceptable. An example would be when the goalkeeper deflects a hard shot towards the corner. In this case, he focuses first on saving the difficult ball, which is the wisest decision he can make. There is very little time to worry about what happens next in situations like this one. There still remains a threat though because the keeper was unable to save the ball completely.

- **Degree 3**: Saving the ball and sending it back to a teammate to start a fast counter attack.

This is the most effective choice a goalkeeper can make. There are some keepers who are too far ahead of themselves though. By that I mean they focus too much on the player they intend to send the ball before they've even made the save.

Needless to say, this can affect the keeper`s ability to actually save the ball. It's important to be one or two steps ahead of the game, whenever possible. But it's also crucial to then focus on the moment, once you have put your future intentions to one side.

These are the three degrees of effectiveness. The decisions a keeper make are determined as good or bad based on these three aspects. There is one other important thing a goalkeeper should consider in difficult situations on the field. He must be ever mindful of timing.

A fast decision that doesn't quite go as expected is better than a late decision. But even a late decision is better than no decision at all, at least in most cases it is. Soccer has not place for indecisiveness.

Think about the following scenario. Let's say a player from the opposite side sends a fast, high ball behind your team's defense line. The ball is in the air and heading toward an attacker who looks set to receive it.

When he does, you will likely get into a one-to-one confrontation with him. Any goalkeeper in this situation will take one of three courses of action. Let's take a look at what those might be.

Goalkeeper 1: He waits until the attacker gets the ball and heads toward his goal with it. This may look like the safer option, but it's often not. This is because 90 percent of breakaways like this end up in a goal for the opposition. So in this case, the goalie's decision will look unreasonable.

Goalkeeper 2: This keeper hesitates and fails to take any decisive action. So in this case the goalie fails to prepare for the attacker. He also fails to distract him by coming out of his goal. Not knowing what to do, and dithering, usually ends in a disastrous outcome.

Goalkeeper 3: This guy moves outside of his penalty area and runs towards the ball and the attacker. In other words, he is competing with the attacker to win possession of the ball.

Maybe he will catch the ball and maybe he won`t, but that's not the main point. What he will succeed in doing is to make it much harder for the attacker to win the ball. And even if the attacker gets the ball, the goalie has still managed to slow him down.

This is a much better option than allowing the opponent to gain possession of the ball and advance toward the goal. Especially when you consider he has more than a 90 percent chance of scoring this way.

As you can see from the three scenarios above, it's obvious that the third reaction is the best one. Despite this, many keepers are hesitant to go out and face attackers outside the penalty area.

The first goalkeeper also has a better chance of making a save than the second. If goalkeeper two did happen to save the shot, it would be out of sheer luck more than anything else.

Keeper number two wasn't able to read the situation well and that's his problem. A goalkeeper's ability to read the situation, and then take quick, decisive action based on his conclusion, is the only way to succeed.

Are you decisive, do you make quick decisions, and are you able to read the situation at hand? If not, it's time to get to work and start improving in these areas.

These are just skills. And like all other skills you can develop them with practice, patience, and by playing in plenty of games. The latter is where experience comes from. Experience is something that can only happen by playing in as many games as possible

12. Guide Your Teammates

Did you know that over 80 percent of the time a team captain will either be a defender or a goalkeeper? This is usually the case in both big and small teams. At Real Madrid, the captain is Spain's defender Sergio Ramos. When he's absent, his goalkeeper Iker Casillas takes over as vice-captain.

In Juventus it's a similar story. Here the team Captain is Italy's goalkeeper, Gianluigi Buffon. And when he is not playing, the captaincy moves to Italy's defender Giorgio Chiellini. At Chelsea, the team`s captain is the defender John Terry. And the vice-captain, after the departure of Frank Lampard, went to goalkeeper, Petr Čech.

There are always a few exceptions to this rule. Sometimes, a player from outside the penalty area becomes the captain of his side. The once Liverpool's midfielder, Steven Gerard, is one example.

Another was the French midfielder, Zinedine Zidane. These "exceptions" had something to do with both players' leadership skills. Their ability to read the game would have also played a part.

Though leadership skills are important, they are not the be-all and end-all of a good captain. So I have included this chapter to show you specifically how a keeper should guide his teammates during a game.

So what do I mean when I say leadership alone is not enough? Well, think about it like this: how could you expect to delegate if you are unable to read the game and predict various situations.

You couldn't, of course. To be a good leader you have to know where to lead from, and the more you know, the better your leadership becomes.

Playing as a goalkeeper, or a defender, puts you in a unique position. By that I mean you have the best possible views of the game of the entire team.

This is something that makes it so much easier for you to read everything. You can also spot things that others fail to see. You get to fix some of the mistakes that your teammates make too.

OK, let's now take a look at your core responsibilities as a goalkeeper/captain. Your ability to guide the team plays a crucial role in determining the outcome of a given situation specifically, and the game more generally.

A Goalkeeper is responsible for the following:

1. Distributing roles among his teammates in all set pieces around the penalty area. This includes corner kicks. It also includes direct and indirect free kicks played outside the area. In these situations, the keeper is the one who gets to see all the opponents inside this zone. It makes perfect sense, therefore, for him to guide his teammates. Here he gets them to cover any unmarked opponents.

2. Distributing roles among his teammates in counter attacks. It's also important to take control of situations where his defense is outnumbered. In these conditions, the goalie is the only one who gets to see any gaps left uncovered. For example, let's say the rival team is performing a counter attack on your side. And let's assume that your defenders are all busy focusing on the player with the ball. With their eyes firmly fixed on the player with the ball they will be unaware of any fast opponents moving up from behind. But you're not! You get to see any players trying to occupy empty spaces as they prepare to receive a pass from the ball holder. This is an invaluable insight. When you alert your players of what is going on, they can then spring into action and do something about it. When a keeper is good at alerting his field players he helps to prevent many dangerous situations from materializing.

Guiding your players means you have to have a strong voice, and not be afraid to use it either. You also need to be effective with body language for times when the players are out of earshot.

Body language can also be useful when you don't want the opponents to know what you're trying to convey to your field players. And finally, you have to be able to read the game well.

This means anticipating various situations. You then need to effectively delegate certain roles to your field players as and when the needs arise.

13. Know How to Deal with Free Kicks

More than third of the goals scored in football result from either a direct foul or a set piece. A set piece, or set play, refers to a situation in soccer when the ball returns to open play following a stoppage.

This might be after a corner or an indirect free kick as two examples. It's imperative that the goalkeeper knows how to react in these situations.

We will look at corners, and how best to deal with them, later in the book. For now though, I want to talk about fouls, and direct free kicks in particular.

Quite often a goal from a free kick happens not because it was well-placed or kicked with great power.

The reason is much more likely to be that the keeper didn't manage his defensive wall too well. Another reason could be that he took the decision to dive too soon. There are three things a goalkeeper needs to be mindful of when it comes to saving free kicks:

1. He has to organize his teammates in a way that makes it harder for the other players to score. That might sound logical, but it's often not done very well. The first thing a goalie needs to get right is his defensive wall. How a keeper organizes his wall shows his level of ability at securing the situation. To do a good job, he first has to organize his teammates according to their height. The tallest player is the last man on the wall. This is so that he can block the corner angle. Once he does that, the goalkeeper will then have to adjust the movement of the wall to the right or to the left. This is to make sure the wall of players covers the far angle or the far corner of the goal. The head of the last player, or the second to last player standing in the wall, should be parallel to the goal's bar. That's the bar of the corner that I'm referring to here.

2. Taking the proper position relative to the wall. In any free kick, the purpose of the wall is to cover the area of the goal that the goalkeeper won't be able to. So always make sure that the goalie and the wall of players never cover the same part of the goal. Instead, one of them covers the right part, while the other covers the left. How this works depends on the side the free kick is played. Right after the keeper organizes his wall, he then has to position himself. This needs to be in a place where he can see the ball as it plays. He also has to be careful not to position himself too far from the far side of the goal. If he does that, he won't be able to save the ball if it passes the wall. How the goalkeeper organizes his wall will vary from one free kick to another. The one thing that must remain constant is to never stand right next to the bar of the goal. If you do this, you increase the distance you have to cover before you dive. It will also kill any chance you have of saving the ball anytime that it passes the wall.

3. Assess the difficulty of play and ask for help on the goal line (if needed). There are situations where you can ask one of your teammates to help you by standing at the far end of your goal. His role here is to clear the ball away if you fail to save it after it passes the wall. This extra help is useful in situations where the player taking the free kick is exceptionally skillful. Another time to call for help might be when the free kick is opposite you and on the edge of the penalty area. You can see some professional teams use this tactic when they play against FC Barcelona. They need all the help they can get when facing free kicks played by Lionel Messi, that's for sure. This guy is famous to the point where he's feared by rivals the world over. In one game against Seville, in the European Super Cup, Messi took four free kicks. Two of them went straight into the net. One other didn`t get past the wall, and the fourth got away from Seville's keeper. This attempt directed the ball toward Barcelona striker Pedro, who then went on to score an easy goal.

This game ended in a 5-4 win for Barcelona. Seville's keeper should have asked one of his teammates to stand on the goal line next to him. If he had of done, they would have more than likely won that game.

OK, let's use the German central defender, Mats Hummels, to illustrate another example of assisting the keeper. By the way, Hummel's is one of the best defenders in Europe at the time of writing.

His team, Borussia Dortmund, was playing against Hoffenheim in the German League in December, 2014. They were facing a dangerous free kick at the time.

Hummels predicted what would happen and left the defense line to race back toward the goal. From there he managed to change the direction of the ball with a fantastic header. This was the "save of the month" in the Bundesliga. If you haven't seen it, I recommend that you go watch it on YouTube.

So these are the basic principles of how to organize your teammates during a foul. Now it's time to learn how to dive with great effect.

I have covered everything you need to know about diving in the following chapter. To give you a hint though, you will always have to take a few steps before you making your jump or dive.

If you don't, you reduce your chances of saving or deflecting the ball by quite a bit. A successful goalkeeper never dives for the sake of it. And he never dives just to make himself look good. Dive only when you need to dive, when the appropriate situation calls for it.

When you dive to save the ball you need your dive to be powerful and well-timed. This is especially true for those balls coming at you from a lethal angle or toward the top corner of the goal. To get the best out of any dive you have to be able to stretch your body to the max.

The more you can stretch, the better your chances are of reaching the ball before it gets too close to your goal. The only way to achieve this is to take a few steps before you launch your jump.

Goalkeepers who jump from the standing still position rarely manage to reach the ball, or if they do it's a weak contact. When this happens, they fail to create enough power in their hands to deflect the ball away from the goal.

Look out for this the next time you watch a soccer game. Even when they do manage to get a touch on the ball from a standing still dive, the ball usually keeps moving. This is because they just haven't generated enough power to make much of an impact.

Remember to dive only when there is no other alternative. Going for a dive in a wrong situation may end up with you hurting yourself. It could also see you concede a silly goal, neither of which are what you would wish for.

14. Know How to Dive

Believe it or not, but a considerable percentage of amateur goalkeepers don't know how to dive. They either fail to use their body's full capabilities or they injure themselves trying.

To become good at diving you have to know where you're current at and then start from there. To do this, see if you can answer any the following five questions before reading my answers:

Question 1: When should you dive? A goalkeeper should dive only when there is no other option. This is not advice that a lot of amateurs heed. Any dive, whether it's necessary or not, carries some risk of potential injury.

So, when a goalkeeper decides to dive, diving should be his only option to save the ball. When a shot is low or parallel to the ground, a keeper should save the ball using his legs or feet.

Quite often he decides to dive, instead. You can see this happen a lot. So despite the fact that his legs and feet are closer to the ball anyway, he opts to dive. It makes no sense at all to dive for a ball that is more savable using an easier and more reliable option.

So the general rule of thumb is this: A keeper should never dive for the ball unless it's too far for him to save or deflect using his hands or legs. That's it in a nutshell.

Question 2: What should you do before you dive?

There are two types of diving. The first one is the instant dive, performed from the standing-still position.

The second is where the goalkeeper takes a few steps before launching into his dive. The latter is the better dive as it allows him to propel his body and stretch to the max. This dive is the non-instant dive.

The difference between these two types of dive is simple. The non-instant dive is more powerful and more effective than the instant dive. Running and jumping does take a bit of practice though.

There's also the safety aspect to consider. One of the things that a keeper has to be careful of is to avoid hitting one of the two bars.

It might sound like a comic sketch, but running face-first or diving into a goalpost is no laughing matter. It will be painful at best and cause serious injury at worse.

It's crucial that you know where you are in relation to all obstructions before taking the run-up to your dives. Once you've done this you can pin your focus on the ball and concentrate on saving it.

One thing you should consider with regards to diving is your height. Goalkeepers who are not so tall (below 1.86m) can rarely play the instant dive.

They just don't have the luxury of reaching higher balls from the standing position. So the shorter keepers have to be quick and use the non-instant dive whenever they can.

Goalkeepers like Thibaut Courtois (1.99m) won't have the "height" issues. Courtois, who plays for Belgium's National team, is huge. This guy can do fingertip saves in his sleep.

Needless to say, he spends a lot less time running and jumping that many others. In general, for goalkeepers who are not super tall, or unusually short, the instant dive is a rarity. They should only use it when the ball requires a quick reflex or when movements are restricted.

Question 3: What hand should you use?

When you dive to catch a ball, especially one that is high and approaching at a lethal angle, always use the hand that is opposite to the direction of the ball. For example, consider a ball that is heading toward the top right corner of your goal.

You're not likely to catch a ball like this, so your aim will be to deflect it away. In this case, it's better and easier for you to use your left hand to make the save.

The reason for this is because this hand corresponds with the movement of your body. This allows you to stretch to the max as you reach for the ball. Unlike your right hand, in this situation, your left hand reaches a much wider range.

Question 4: How can you to give yourself a mental boost to help reach the ball?

A good goalkeeper is strong, flexible and mentally prepared. He knows how to condition his mind so that he's in the right headspace by the time a game starts.

When it comes to making dives, especially ambitious dives, you have to believe in the outcome. In other words, you have to think that you WILL save that ball, and not think that you will TRY to save it.

Approaching a dive with commitment and conviction will reinforce your positive mindset. This in turn gives you a good mental boost.

Likewise, if you have any doubt, even a tiny smidgen of doubt, the reverse is true. Even if you're capable of saving the ball, from a physical perspective, you can still fail if you have any self-doubt.

Question 5: How can I land to avoid injury?

Always consider where you are in relation to the nearest bar or any other obstruction. Make this quick assessment before doing any dives.

Too many goalies track the ball or dive without considering where they are relative to where the nearest bar is. It's a bad habit and one that can, and sometimes does, see the keeper get hurt or injured.

The other thing to keep in mind when diving for the ball is not the dive itself but the fall back to the ground. Again, if you land wrong you can get hurt or injured.

You especially want to avoid falling smack down onto your ribs or your back. Seriously, you don't want to fall hard onto your bones, believe me.

Instead, you need to fall on an area of your body that has some meat on it. We all have places that have a little more muscle and fat.

Protection is one of the reasons the body stores fat. The name for this is mechanical cushioning. Without it, we would always be hurting ourselves as we would be all bone.

So the best way to land and avoid injury is to use your arms. You can also land on your thighs. Either way, you land on the hip side, which is by far the safest way to hit the deck. If you feel your shorts and goalkeeper's shirt, you will notice how the material used at the thigh and elbows is different.

The fabric is more protective for safety reasons. If you're a novice right now, then you might want to look for goalkeeper pants with the most protection.

Another way to land safe is by using the ball. When you catch the ball in the air, you can then use it to help cushion your landing.

15. Take Responsibility for Each Goal and Every Mistake

Lost goals and keeper mistakes might seems like catastrophes at the time they occur. Of course, no one wants to fail, but we all do, sometimes. What's more is that without these failures we would learn nothing. The best goalkeepers in the world have all had their failures and setbacks along the way.

In fact, they would never have reached their levels of excellence without some failures. So failure isn't your enemy, it's your friend. Any failure to change is the only time failure becomes a problem.

But when you learn from your disappointments you get to grow. The biggest failure of all is the failure to try. So try to view failure as your teacher, not your undertaker.

"I have not failed. I've just found 10,000 ways that won't work." ~ Thomas A. Edison

The quote above from the American inventor and businessman, Thomas Edison, is so true. When we look at failure in a constructive way, as opposed to a destructive way, we find out what doesn't work, and that can only be a good thing. The former British Prime Minister, Winston Churchill, once said this of failure:

"Success is stumbling from failure to failure with no loss of enthusiasm."

As a goalkeeper you must show interest in good results. Results are rarely automatic. They usually come about from hard work, commitment, patience and persistence.

You also achieve you best results by a willingness to learn from your failures. Don't beat yourself up for failing. And never put yourself down in front of others when you fail in goal. Defeatist attitudes always hurt, not help, a goalkeeper development.

All keepers feel bad when they concede a goal, and that's understandable. But when they fail to take responsibility for it they cannot learn or develop. This way they give in to failure, when in fact they should embrace it. Blaming something or someone else for the goal is not helpful. It doesn't help you, and it doesn't help your team.

Instead, you should try to identify why that ball got past you and then make sure it doesn't happen again. At least try to make sure there's no repeat of the same slip up because "try" is all you can expect of yourself.

To every problem there is a solution. But you can only apply a solution once you know what the problem is. For example, if you let a goal in, rather than blame someone or something else for that, try to see why it happened.

What was the "real" reason? Maybe you dived too early. In that case, you can tell yourself you will be more careful of this future and try your best not to let it happen again.

Taking responsibility for everything that happens to you requires a shift in mindset. For some reason, soccer players, in general, seem to find this hard. There's likely to be a bit of ego involved in there somewhere too. But know this: the highest achievers in life take full responsibility for their actions, or inactions, as the case may be.

There will always be someone scoring goals against you in soccer, no matter how good you are. This is a simple fact that will never change. Some goals are not savable whereas others are. The latter types are the only ones you need to concern yourself with.

It is only when you take responsibility for yourself that you can work on improving your skills. When you hold yourself responsible for any poor performances, something positive happens.

You find yourself performing better at the next game. Being responsible makes you train harder, catch more crosses, and dive with more precision. In short, you demand more from yourself because you are eager to improve. You act this way because you don't want a repeat of past failures.

When you don't hold yourself responsible for any poor performances, something negative happens. In this case, you don't strive to improve. This is because you don't see that you are at fault.

Most of the time, there will be something that YOU did, or didn't do, that allowed the ball to pass the goal line. If you can't see that, then you are in denial mode.

Denial is one of the most common defense mechanisms that many players use, at least to some extent. Denial is when you pretend that an uncomfortable thing did not happen. But it actually did. The problem is that we can end up believing ourselves, and that's a hard habit to break. Denial becomes a convenient cop-out.

As a goalkeeper, you are not only responsible for yourself. You also need to be responsible for the field players, especially the defensive ones. It is your job to guide them often and with great effect.

The role of goalkeeper is an important one. With it comes a lot of accountability. It is a position that you have to own if you are to excel.

Embrace the challenges, and admit when you are wrong. When you fix any shortcomings you might have, you then get to enhance your playing skills. This will also help to improve your leadership skills and earn you respect from the team.

Aspire to be these things and you become a serious contender for the team's captaincy. All this and more can happen with a single shift in focus and obligation.

Below is a quote from Ralph Fulsom Marston, who is a successful player in the American NFL. It is quite an apt way to end this chapter:

"Concern yourself more with accepting responsibility than with assigning blame. Let the possibilities inspire you more than the obstacles discourage you."

16. The Six Second Rule

This is by far the easiest and silliest mistake a goalkeeper can make, not least because it is so unnecessary.

It happens when a goalkeeper holds the ball, either in one hand or both, for too long. The time limit is just six seconds. When the keeper does this he's in trouble. In the past, goalkeepers could not take more than four steps while holding the ball. The six-second rule has since replaced that.

Here's how it works: the referee calls for an indirect free kick inside the penalty area whenever the goalkeeper holds onto the ball for six seconds or more. The danger is that eight out of every ten indirect free kicks played from inside the penalty area translate into goals.

So any goalie who makes this mistake is giving the other team an easy goal on a silver platter. Most referees actually wait for nine or ten seconds before they call a foul.

It should only be six, but few jump on the case quite so soon. Be that as it may, you should never rely on the longer duration. Always assume you only have six seconds at best before moving the ball on.

There's another mistake with consequences like the six second rule. This is when the goalkeeper grabs or touches the ball with any of his hands when one of his teammates passes it to him using his foot.

This is an infringement known as back-pass rule violation. In this case, the referee will again call for an indirect free kick inside the penalty area.

The reason to give these two free kicks in the above situations is to make the game more exciting and less defensive. These rules came about to prevent the goalkeeper from hogging the ball for too long. In the past, he might do this to buy time or to delay the play on purpose.

This time-wasting was useful when the keeper's team was leading in the score. The longer he held the ball back, the less chance the opposition had to equalize or beat the winning side. FIFA created these new rules right after the 1990 World Cup in Italy. Keep reading to find out why.

That tournament saw one of the most unexciting in modern soccer. It was game between Egypt and Ireland, if you can call it a game. Both FIFA and soccer fans alike called it the most boring event in the history of the World Cup.

The score ended at 0-0. Both the Egyptian and the Irish team were happy to maintain a draw. So when either side got the opportunity, they would pass the ball over toward their keepers.

They did this for no other reason than to waste time and prevent the other side from scoring. The goalies would hold the ball in their hands for 15 or 20 seconds a time before throwing it back into play. This might not sound long, but when it happens over and over, it feels like a lifetime of inaction.

To give you some idea of the boredom factor, you only have to look at the post-game statistics. They showed that the Egyptian goalkeeper, Ahmed Shobeir, had the most touches on the ball of all the 22 players.

That's quite unbelievable when you think about it. Well, this can never happen again because of the new rules.

17. How to Save Fouls Played Inside the Penalty Area

Whenever the referee calls an indirect free kick on you because you have violated the 6-second rule, you have to do two things.

The first thing you need to do is gather all your teammates on the goal line. In this case, the referee can't order your teammates to move back 10 yards.

This is because the foul will be inside the penalty area. Usually, the space between the place of the foul and the wall of players remains empty.

In this situation that is not possible because your teammates have to stand on the goal line.

When organizing your wall, all you need to do is to ask the tallest of the players to stand right next to the goal's bar. The reason for this is because it's the place where the majority of these types of foul aim at.

Once the foot of the opponent touches the ball you have to spring into action. Get ready to throw your body to the front, not to the side, as if you are trying to block a pass, not make a dive.

According to mathematics and trigonometry, this is your best chance to save the ball. In this situation, try to think like an American football defender.

He would try to block a kick using his body and hands, and this should be your approach too.

18. Know How to Play Headers

Every soccer goalkeeper should be familiar with, and quite good at, the basics plays of the game. By "basic plays" I mean dribbling, running with the ball, crossing, and sending accurate long passes. He also needs to be good at shooting using both his head and his feet.

In modern soccer the competition is always fierce. The roles and expectations of all players are forever changing. Players nowadays should expect to be more versatile than ever before.

Today, coaches look not only for a good keeper but a complete one. To be "complete" means you can play as well as you can save. It's a tall order, but it's the way it is now.

A great keeper also has good header skills. If he doesn't, then he's not great. He might still be good, but he won't be great. If you're ambitious, then never settle for being just good or okay.

There are two situations where it's especially useful for a keeper to use headers, so let's take a look at those now.

Scenario 1: A player from the other side sends a long through ball behind your team's defensive line. The ball is in the air and traveling toward the opposite team's striker. Since the ball is outside the penalty area, you can only use your head or your feet.

In this case you will use your head to clear the ball away, before it reaches the other player. If the ball gets to the rival striker before you get to it, then he has an easy chance to score against your team.

Scenario 2: Your team is one goal behind in the score and you're playing in stoppage time. Your team is then awarded a corner or a serious free kick on the right or the left side of the opposite team's penalty area.

Since you are already one goal behind you've got nothing to lose here. This means you can be a bit more daring than usual. You can consider running toward the opposite team's penalty area, as a way to add an extra player to your sides attacking force.

Once there, you could try your luck with a header or a kick. Or at the very least, you assist your teammates by forcing one of the other team's players to mark you. Either way, by playing or distracting, you're making a valuable contribution.

Here's a real-world demonstration of this.

I was watching a game between PSV Eindhoven, my favorite team in the Netherlands. They were playing the Dutch side, Ado Den Haag FC, in the Dutch league, Eredivisie. The Eredivisie is the highest echelon of professional football in Holland.

The league itself was founded in 1956, just two years after the start of professional football in that country.

During the game, Eindhoven was leading the score at 2-1 until the ninety-fifth minute. Then Ado Den Haag got a free kick on the left side of the penalty area.

Since he had nothing to lose, Den Haag`s goalkeeper, Martin Hansen, made a bold decision. He left his goal and went to join his teammates in Eindhoven`s penalty area.

The free kick was played low and came toward Hansen. This is when he got to show his true ability as a complete player. Hansen flipped around and kicked a difficult ball with his back heel, straight toward Eindhoven's goal.

He scored, which gave his team a late equalizer. By scoring that spectacular goal he's certain to get a nomination for the FIFA 2015 goal of the year award.

19. Know How to Catch a Corner

A goalkeeper who is good at catching corner kicks, crosses and high balls is worth his weight in gold. He's becomes one of the most important assets any team can have, though a keeper like this is something of a rarity. Get good at these things and teams will be fighting over you.

Imagine how secure and calm a side becomes when they have a keeper who can catch most of the high balls he receives. If you need to improve in this area, here are six things to keep in mind when attempting to save a corner.

1. **Make sure your path is clear**. Inform the referee whenever a player from the opposite team is restricting your movement. It's important that your make sure it is clear for you to take a jump so you can catch the corner kick. You must also make sure that the tallest of your teammates, usually the two center backs, are close to you. These guys have to prevent any rival players from distracting you as you leave the goal and go in for the save.

2. **Make sure that you estimate the effects of the wind**. I discuss the various effects of the weather later in the book. For now though, understand the changes that can happen on windy days. The wind can disrupt both the speed and the direction of the ball. How much disruption there is clearly depends on the wind. Too much wind makes it difficult for a keeper to catch a cross in particular. There is a secret to succeeding in windy situations, as you wait for the cross. That is, you must slow yourself down a bit. Certainly take more time than in normal conditions. In other words, don't rush in. You need to wait until you can predict the direction of the ball. On blustery days, a ball can end up somewhere quite different to where you first thought it was heading. Get to read the wind and you will be more successful in these situations.

3. **Bend (raise) one knee when taking off.** There will be times when there are just too many players around as you prepare to jump for a cross or a corner kick. In these situations, it's far better and much safer to bend one of your knees as you take off from the ground. Bending the knee gives you extra power for the jump. It allows you to reach higher and move faster, thus increasing your chances to punch or catch the ball. This way of jumping in crowded situations also prevents rival players from distracting or hurting you while you're up in the air. To perform the jump, raise the knee nearest any opposing pressure as you jump up. This way you give yourself some protection or distance, from any onrushing forwards, as well as a boost for the jump. You should never raise the knee with intent to injure or even send a warning to another player. The main purpose for the raised knee is to generate more height on the jump first. The second purpose is to act as a kind of fender against collisions.

4. **Always keep the two shortest players next to you.** Ask the shortest two players on your team to assist you. They don't have to be defenders. Just get them to stand on the goal line, right next to the goal bars. What this will do is help you to stay more focused on the ball. This is because you are now in charge of only two thirds of the goal instead of covering the whole thing.

5. **Beware of corners played outside the box**. Corners played away from the box can be tricky to say the least. This is because they delude the goalkeeper, often tricking him into going after the ball. And as he does, he then realizes that the ball is too far away for him to reach. Whoops! His goal is now wide open and unprotected. In moments of hesitancy like this the goalkeeper finds that he is lost and uncertain. He's in a kind of no-man's land, too far away to reach the ball, yet too far away to defend his goal. Think quickly and act fast by all means, but never do so before weighing up the situation.

6. **Always allow room for moving backwards (backpedaling)**. Sometimes the player taking the corner kick will get lucky and his ball will go toward the goal's far post. In this situation, the keeper should in a position where he can move backwards at a moment's notice. If he's not, he won't be able to secure the far post and catch the ball or clear it away toward the corner. To prepare for this, the goalie needs to take a quick look behind to see if the area is clear. Just running back without checking first can, and often does, result in a collision. You have to be aware of your surroundings to make informed safe, decisions. In these situations, the keeper should also avoid jumping from his standing position. It is better to move back a couple of steps to improve the chances of reaching the ball.

20. Use Both Hands and Legs Equally

Some keepers have difficulty catching balls or punching them away with their non-prominent hand. Others have problems using their non-prominent foot. And there are some keepers who just can't work with either their non-prominent foot or their hand.

Whether you do or don't use your non-prominent side determines your success. Those who don't use their non-prominent sides are more likely untrained rather than unable.

What I mean by that is there's a good chance they could use their weaker side if only they had worked on it. Yes it takes time, and yes it can be awkward to get used to it. But it's not an impossible task, not for those who are willing to put in the time and effort.

I'm assuming you want to be the best goalkeeper that you can be. If I'm right, that means you have to be able to use all parts of your body if you're to reach a level of greatness.

Why drive a car on three wheels when it has four. The more tricks and tools you have at your disposal, the more you get to do.

Think about all the extra saves you can make if you can bring either arm or leg into play. You double your options, so it makes perfect sense to develop your weak side.

The point here is this: being able to use either hand or foot to make saves will skyrocket your ability to succeed in goal.

Here are some ways that will help you to strengthen and develop your non-prominent leg.

Drill 1

To help the keeper develop his non-prominent leg, some coaches use a simple "no-hands" exercise. The method is to force the goalkeeper to use his feet to save low shots close to his body. Using hands to save the ball is not allowed, no matter how practical it may seem.

If the keeper can't break the habit of using his hands, the coach will have an answer for that too. He restricts the keeper`s movements by tying his hands together. This then forces the goalie to use his feet and legs to save every ball. It's a simple but effective approach.

Like training for any new skill, the only way to get good at it is by repetition. With the above drill, the keeper should complete 50 saves per session without using his hands. Some guys don't like the idea of having their hands tied up for safety reasons.

In this case, every time he fails to use his feet and saves with his hands, the coach ads 10 more saves to the session. This negative form of reinforcement is a great way to keep any goalie focused.

For this exercise to succeed, it's important to replicate real situations. This means the one firing the shots at the goal has to play every ball low and aim close to the keeper's body.

These are the types of saves which use the legs, so these are the ones to use for the drill. The shooter also needs to come in from the wings (right or left) as he approaches the goal.

If you practice and master this technique, I can guarantee you will be so much more successful. To start with, you will improve in one-to-one situations. And you will also fare much better when an attacker plays a low ball at close range.

Drill 2

Another thing goalkeepers should do is have a steady leg stretching routine. This enables you to increase the area you cover with your legs.

A keeper should also add some strengthening exercises to his workouts. These will not only strengthen and improve leg and feet movements, but they will also help to reduce the risk of injury while playing in goal.

Leg stretching exercises are those where you spread the legs as wide as possible while keeping the toes up. It's better to do leg-stretching exercises after a light jog, or after warming up with squats, lungs and jumping jacks.

When performing leg-stretching exercises, you should feel a slight pull in your legs. If you feel pain then you're going too far and opening your legs too wide.

The best approach is to start slow and gentle. There are many accidents by keepers trying to do too much too soon, so make sure you take it easy. You can always crank things up once you get to know your limits.

Let's now look at how to perform these leg-stretching exercises.

Start by sitting on the ground and opening your legs to the sides until you feel a slight pull. This is your start position.

Now lean forward, slowly, and stop just when you feel the stretch in your legs become intense. Once you're in this position, hold it for 20 or 30 seconds, if you can, before returning to the start position.

The next part of this leg-stretching exercise uses the same start position. This time, instead of leaning forward you turn and lean toward your left foot while trying to touch your toes with your right hand.

Once you're there, or as near as you can get, hold the position for 20 or 30 seconds. You then alternate sides, this time repeating the exercise by touching the toes on your right foot using your left hand.

Once you do this cycle of three exercises, take 20 seconds rest and repeat for 2-3 more cycles. To get yourself limbered up, do this routine every day for five consecutive months. After five months you will be so much more agile.

This means you will be able to cover more area with your legs when using them to save low balls that are close to your body.

You don't have to continue with these leg-stretching exercises every day after the five months is up. But you will want to do them quite regularly nonetheless. This is so that you can maintain the strength and flexibility that you have built up in your legs.

21. Stop Thinking of Who to Pass the Ball to Before Catching It

Easy, slow balls can be the most dangerous that a keeper faces. This is not because they are hard, it's because they are easy, too easy, in fact.

What happens is that the goalie becomes complacent and let's his guard down. There is nothing quite as embarrassing than seeing an easy ball cross over your goal line.

Make sure you never make the mistake of underestimating a slow, easy ball. What usually happens is that the goalie becomes so sure that he will save the ball that he shifts his attention. In other words, he loses his focus on the ball and starts placing it on his next moves.

This will be something like which player to pass the ball to once he gets it. Or whether he should launch a fast counter attack, etc.

As he does this, he forgets about the ball he is so sure about saving. All these things happen in nanoseconds, but then that's all it takes.

So, what happens next?

The keeper fails to catch or deflect the ball. It then either crosses the goal line or it deflects toward his nearest opponent. Whichever one happens, it is bad news either way.

There are a couple of things you can do to save yourself from this embarrassing situation. The first is to treat all balls equal. You should remove the phrase "easy save" from your vocabulary. From now on you have to look at every ball as a potential threat, and I do mean every ball.

There are some professional goalkeepers who let balls into their goal that a toddler could have stopped. And what happens? They became famous for their blunder.

Imagine that, years of playing great soccer at the professional level and people remember you most for letting in a silly goal at an important game.

Ask any goalie who has ever made one of these embarrassing mistakes what they think. They will all say how they wished they could turn back the clocks of time and fix things.

A team can be quite forgiving, but the fans can be a hard lot to please. In fact, fans will never forget, even though some of them might forgive.

OK, so remember to treat all balls as potential threats and never let your guard down. Follow this advice and you will better protect yourself from these awful, unnecessary situations.

The second thing a keeper should do is watch out for a wandering mind. This is not the same thing as consciously thinking about something else.

A wandering mind is when uninvited thoughts come into the forefront of your mind and distract you. Anytime you start thinking about anything other than the ball, or the game in hand, is a potential danger.

A wandering mind is a threat to keepers more so than the field players. This is especially true when a team in dominating and keeping the action far away from their goal.

Since the goalkeeper is the only player to spend the majority of his time alone, it's easy to see how his mind might start to drift.

22. Figure out Where the Goal Ends

Picture this: A player sends a not so hard shot toward the goal. The keeper sees it coming but thinks it's going toward the end line so he doesn't try to save it.

He mistakenly thinks the ball will go out for a goal kick, but it doesn't. Instead, the ball hits the net and it's a goal for the opposition.

This happens more than you might think. In fact, I saw it happen as I was writing this book. I was watching a game one evening in the African Champions League. There was this shot heading towards one of the goals.

This particular goalie thought the ball was going out but he was wrong. The ball went in instead. His team lost 1-0, despite dominating the game for the entire 90 minutes.

The reason behind this mistake was that the goalkeeper was unaware of his exact position relative to the goal.

This happens a lot when a keeper stands on his goal line thinking he is covering the right angle or taking the right position.

So, how can you make sure this doesn`t happen to you?

The answer is simple. Follow every ball until you either save it or watch it cross the end line.

Don't ever leave a shot assuming it`s going out without first checking your position and that of the goal. It's an easy mistake to make, but it can cause a lot of upset if you're not aware of it.

23. How to Stay Motivated and Hungry

To be a successful goalkeeper you need passion, ambition, patience and a great deal of hard work. For every one great player there are thousands of others who never make the grade. Many of those will be good, very good in some cases, but not quite good enough.

Every player who made his name into your memory had something special to offer. Even the B+ players have something that helps them to stand out from the pack. What all these players have in common is their unyielding commitment to succeed.

They never give up, no matter what or who stands in their way. No one can put them off by telling them they're not good enough. If anyone tries to tell them they can't succeed, they become even more committed, never less.

The big money that's associated with professional soccer attracts a lot of young players. It's true that some of soccer's greats become super wealthy, but money should never be your primary focus. In actual fact, money can be a distraction.

If you want to play professional soccer because of the money, then you never will. It always has to be about the game first. Anything else is just a bonus. Money alone will never motivate you enough to become a soccer superstar. Only passion, dedication, patience, persistence and a genuine love for the game can do that.

The demand for talented players is a lot less than the supply. There will be tens of thousands of young players the world over who all aspire to reach the big time. But there will only ever be a tiny handful of available slots in professional soccer to accommodate a few. So the competition is tough, to put it mildly.

Only the best of the best will stand a chance. Talent scouts look for passion and potential. They can spot things in players that other can't see, even the players themselves. People are often surprised at how a lesser talented player is sometimes picked over the most talented.

It's because the scout saw something in that player that set him apart. Never underestimate potential. Some good goalkeepers might have reached their potential. Others might still have plenty of growth left. Talent scouts are good at spotting these things.

If fame and fortune motivates you, then you will never stand out. Goalkeeping has to be in your blood. You live and breathe it.

You can't get enough of the #1 position. When you're not playing in goal you're thinking about playing in goal.

You love the game so much that others not only see this in you, but they feel it from you too. Passion oozes out of your every pore. People love to watch you play because you have that "special something."

If you love the thought of money and material gains more than the game itself, then you are dreaming the wrong dream.

To succeed in soccer you need both physical and mental toughness. You need to be able to pick yourself up and push through setbacks and injuries. You have to be strict about your exercises routines.

You must maintain both your physical strength and your physical fitness at all times. This means that late night parties and going out on the town with friends become something a rarity during the soccer season.

You cannot let pain, disappointments, criticisms and failure get to you. You need to be able to raise above all negative influences. In other words, to be a great goalkeeper you have to grow the skin of a rhinoceros.

Confidence is a must-have quality. If you don't believe in yourself then neither will others. You never boast or praise yourself up, telling folks how great you are. If you're that good, other people will spread the message for you. Anyone who feels the need to brag is not as good as they think they are.

If they were, they wouldn't have to keep telling folks. In fact, others would be telling him how good he is, and thanking him for his contribution to the team.

Look deep inside yourself and question your motives. Maybe you want to play for the best clubs in the world. Then again, perhaps you just want to make a reasonable living playing for a smaller team. Whichever it is, question your reasons why. Is it the game, the glory, the money?

You should want to play for the love of the game. But for you to progress you have to be hungry for success. This is not something you can fake. Find out the real reasons why you want to play in goal and write them down. Hopefully they will read the right way. When you have done this, pin those reasons up somewhere so that you can always see them.

To summarize this chapter:

To be a "great" goalkeeper you need passion and skill. You actually need a wide variety of skills. You have to be a motivational teammate.

You can organize plays, and hinder/obstruct attacks that could otherwise be shots at your goal. You must have good mental and physical strength.

You must also maintain peak physical fitness at all times. A good goalkeeper has leadership skills. The difference between winning and losing a soccer match often lies with the goalie. Be the one.

24. Stay Focused When the Ball Is Not Around

You must maintain a strong focus during the game. You cannot allow anything to distract you throughout the entire 90-120 minutes. It can be easy to get distracted in goal though, that's if you allow it to happen.

Anytime you let yourself lose focus while the game is on, you risk putting yourself and your team in danger.

Soccer is a fast moving game that needs quick thinking and speedy reflexes. Neither of these is achievable when your mind is elsewhere. Let's look at a real example to illustrate this point better.

I was watching a game between the English teams Arsenal and West Ham United. It was the first game in the English Premier League and Arsenal was dominating.

I would say that Arsenal had possession of the ball 60-70 percent of the time. Despite their dominance, Arsenal still failed to win the game. In fact, they wasted more than 14 serious scoring opportunities.

The final score was 2-0 to West Ham United. So how could something like this happen when Arsenal managed to dominate the game?

Well, it was because one of their team members' let the side down. In a team sport like soccer, it only takes one weak link in the chain to disrupt the team effort.

The weakest link in this game was Arsenal`s goalkeeper, Petr Čech. He lost his focus on two occasions during the game. The first time was when he let in a goal from a free kick.

The second was when a ball he wasn't expecting came in from a dead angle. The second shot, in particular, should have been so easy for a great keeper like Čech to save. But on this day he couldn't save either of these balls because he had momentarily lost his focus.

So how did this happen, what caused Čech to lose his concentration? It was most likely the result of being out of the action for too long.

It's great when your team is dominating a game, but it also means the keeper doesn't get to see much action. These are the times when a goalkeeper is most at risk of losing his focus.

There is a simple trick that helps a keeper maintain his focus in these situations. All he has to do is to imagine he's the goalie of the weaker side. This is because when your team dominates a game, the other keeper sees all the action.

Your solution for maintaining focus is to imaging what you would do in the other goalkeeper's situation. How would you save the shots that are attacking his goal? In other words, you put yourself in his shoes. By doing this you get to keep your mind focused firmly on the game, albeit in a different way.

What this method does is keep your mind sharp and your enthusiasm high. Although you're not involved in the game in a physical sense, you are still engaged in it mentally, and that's the point.

This is by far a better approach than letting your mind wander. The only thing you should be thinking about during the game is the game itself. This simple method allows you to do just that.

25. Change Your Position on the Goal Line

You need to change your position on the goal line so that you can follow the rapid movements of the ball.

One of the main responsibilities of a goalkeeper is to track the ball wherever it goes. To do this he has to keep switching positions according to the ball's movement. This ensures he is in the right place to save the ball at the right time.

It also allows him to cover the right angles so that he is in the best position to save the ball from wherever it comes at him.

The goalkeeper should not move horizontally across his goal line. This approach opens up too many angles for the opponents to shoot at.

Whenever the ball is outside the penalty area, the keeper should move on an imaginary semicircle. Think of this as one that connects both sides of the goal and you will get the idea.

It just means a line that starts from the one bar and swoops round to the other. This imaginary line is the best way for a goalkeeper to move. It allows him to follow the ball wherever it is, at all times.

He couldn't do this by moving horizontally along his goal line. This is definitely the best approach whenever the ball is moving around the field at a fast pace, as is often the case.

You need to cover the widest possible area when tracking the ball. Moving around your goal like this is the only way to do that effectively. This approach also makes it harder for the opponents to score as you get to cover all the angles better.

26. Take Notice of Opponents Moving Around You

Here are three typical scenarios to illustrate what happens when a goalkeeper is unaware of his opponent's location.

Let's say a ball is in play around the penalty area. The keeper then decides to leave his goal to go and save it.

As he does this, an opponent appears out of nowhere and snatches the ball from under the goalie's nose. In many situations like this, the opponent then goes on to score.

The above situation is one that happens all too often.

Another "surprise attack" is when the keeper drops the ball to the ground and prepares to kick it. Again, he is unaware of the nearby opponent who then appears out of nowhere.

That opponent then snatches the ball and scores an easy goal straight into the empty net.

And the third common situation is when the keeper is about to punt the ball. In this case, the nearby opponent waits for the goalkeeper to release the ball with his hands.

Just as he does, the opponent rushes in and steals the ball with a single swipe of his leg, sending it straight into an empty net.

All these situations are avoidable. That is providing you always take note of where your opponents are in relation to where you are.

27. Become Familiar with the Other Team's Game Play

Being able to predict where the next ball will play, or who it will likely receive it, is a skill. It's something that all the most successful goalies learn to do.

To be able to do this well, the keeper has to be familiar with the playing style of the rival team. The more he knows about them, the easier it for him to read the game.

If you study professional soccer games (recommended), you will notice one thing that's consistent.

You will see how most teams, or players, rarely change their playing style. Or at least they don't make any dramatic changes to the way they play.

The majority of coaches base their teams` tactics and playing style on two things. The first is the strengths and weaknesses of each player.

The second is the strengths and weaknesses of the team. He then puts together his side based on these observations.

Even as players come and go, a team's style of play rarely changes. This is especially true when they are successful more often than not. As the old adage goes:

"If it's not broken, don't try to fix it."

Most British teams tend to play highly physical soccer. It is a style that typically depends on high balls. Because of this, their main strikers are usually those with the best header skills.

Teams like Stoke City, for example, tend to play a lot of crosses. This requires a special approach, especially for corners and set pieces. Here the opponents have to deal with at least five players who are strong, good at headers, and above 1.88m in height.

Teams like Barcelona, on the other hand, require their goalkeeper to be in a continuous state of motion. This is because he needs to track the ball at all times.

The playing style of Barcelona is to rotate the ball a lot. That means their keeper has to be in a state of constant monitoring for him to be successful.

The point here is that all teams play soccer by the soccer rules, but they don't all play the same style.

When playing competitive soccer you can't afford to be unfamiliar with the other team's style. If you're serious about winning, then you need to spend some time studying the rival side before game day.

There are lots of ways to do this. Going to see them play live, or watching videos are the best. The latter is usually the preferred approach. With video, you get to pause, rewind, and replay bits of the game that are of most interest to you.

The goalkeeper is often the one to guide his teammates. This is especially the case with the defensive players. He has to communicate and regroup his team to cover all possible threats.

The more he knows about the team he's up against, the better his team's chances are of beating them.

28. Become Familiar with the Other Team's Best Striker

Let's assume you have done your homework and gotten yourself familiar with the different tactics and playing style of the rival team.

Your next job is to focus on the key player's. You will want to pay particular attention to their main striker, or their leading goal scorer.

In any team, there will be two or three key players. These are the guys who are responsible for creating and scoring 80 percent of their team's goals.

They are the players who you need to focus on the most. Let's take a look at how you might go about studying them.

The first thing you will want to identify is patterns. All good, consistent players have set patterns that they use. Sometimes you will come across a player whose style is unpredictable, but most are not.

So you need to try and identify any repetitive behavior in the key players. The only way to do this is to watch them perform in different games.

OK, let's take a professional player to illustrate the point.

Arjen Robben is a talented Dutch winger who plays for FC Bayern at the time of writing. Robben has a predicable style that goes something like this:

He runs along the right flank and then suddenly goes deeper into the field before firing a strong shot toward the far post of the goal. He rarely crosses and he rarely passes.

This is a style of play that he never fails to perform whenever he gets the slightest opportunity.

Let's see what you can learn from these repeated patterns. So you know how and where Robben likes to play his balls and fire his shots.

Because of this, you are in a better position to do something about it. To keep his balls out of your goal depends on your position relative to the goal, as well as the speed of the shot.

Knowing what Robben's moves are likely to be puts you in a much better position to defeat him. Of course you won't be able to stop all his attempts.

But you will be more in control of defending your goal now that you know what to expect. Knowledge and preparation are by far your best weapons for protecting your goal.

Get into the habit of studying rival teams and their best players. It is something that is well worth the time as you will discover.

29. Know How to Deal with Balls That Bounce off the Ground

It's never a good feeling when you throw yourself to the ground in an attempt to catch a ball, only to then see it bounce off course before it reaches you.

Bouncing balls do happen, and whether you save them or not depends on how prepared you are. The way to prepare for bouncing balls is by working on your reflexes.

When you have good reflexes you get to act fast and without any conscious thought. The best exercises for these types of balls are with the help of your coach or a teammate. The first one is simple in theory but not so easy to master in practice. You do need an assistant though.

In your training session, get someone to stand close to you with a few balls at the ready. They should be about 7-10 yards away.

The job of the assistant is to throw the balls hard in your direction. But instead of sending them toward you directly through the air, ask the assistant to strike them with force on the ground, so that they bounce. Get the assistant to perform a lot throws and from all possible directions. If you can, do 100 or 200 for each training session. It won't take too long before you notice a marked improvement in how quick you react to these bouncing balls.

Once you start to get good with this technique, it's then time to up the challenge a bit. This time, get your assistant to perform the same type of throws by using different sized balls. This will challenge your skills to a higher level.

Using different sized balls makes this exercise a lot more difficult (only move on to this drill after you have mastered the first one). You will want to include tennis balls, baseball balls, and footballs, among others of varying sizes. Note that the more you train on smaller and faster balls, the better your performance will get.

There is another exercise that you will want to incorporate into your training program. This one helps to improve your skills for more unpredictable bounces. To begin this exercise, start by placing any number of objects on the ground.

These will want to be both inside and outside the penalty area, but not too far from it. These objects need placing on the ground at various angles too. This way, whenever the ball hits them, the direction it goes in will be more unpredictable.

OK, so your assistant starts to kick some of the balls at you directly. He also kicks others so that they bounce off those inclined objects placed around the field. He doesn't forewarn you of his intention. This helps to keep you alert.

Not knowing how one ball arrives from the next creates a surprises element. This is to better replicate how things are likely to occur in real games. This exercise is quite tricky so make sure you practice the first two drills before tackling this one.

Once you get good as this exercise, your ability to save bouncing galls will improve hugely. That's provided you get in plenty of practice of course.

Be Aware of the Surface

One of the most overlooked observations is that of the field. It's important that you become familiar with the state of the ground before a game.

This is especially important around your goal area. The condition of a soccer field can have a huge impact on how the game plays out.

For example, a patchy field with dips and holes all over the place, even small ones, means one thing. It means the direction of the ball becomes more unpredictable after hitting it.

A field that is even and has a well-cared for grassy surface, on the other hand, means the balls which hit it will be more predictable.

Most of the time, a goalkeeper will be able to predict and save a bouncy ball just by keeping himself aware of the condition of the field around his goal area.

Forewarned is forearmed, as they say. This awareness will force the keeper to be more cautious before taking any dives. He will also think more carefully before stretching his body to catch balls.

In an ideal world, all soccer fields would have the perfect surface, and all game days would have the perfect weather.

In the real world, however, we know this is just wishful thinking. So getting familiar with various conditions before a game is something which all savvy keepers do.

30. Know How to Play in Different Weather Conditions

Every extreme weather condition adds a certain type of difficulty for any goalkeeper. An experienced goalie prepares to play in all types of weather, and under all circumstances.

Playing on Wet or Rainy Days

Playing on a wet or rainy day means the soccer ball will be heavier than usual. That requires strikers to exert more power to achieve the same effect, when compared to a more normal, dry day.

Whether it's a direct shot, a cross, or a high ball, the keeper's job is one heck of a lot harder whenever the ball becomes sodden.

Any striker who is smart enough to exploit a wet game usually gets the upper hand. He is the one who anticipates mistakes. This is the guy who is always ready to retake any ball that the goalie fails to grasp.

In wet conditions, it`s better that the keeper relies more on punching the ball away than catching it. This approach is particular beneficial for high balls. It's also better to deflect the ball to either side of the goal than it is trying to control or catch it in the rain.

Rainy days also need a higher level of concentration from the keeper. And the more it rains, the more he has to pay attention. The worse the weather gets, the harder it becomes to see.

It goes without saying that a keeper's best chance of saving any ball is when he can see it coming. If the color of the ball is gray or white, the keeper's job of tracking it in the rain becomes even more difficult.

No one relishes playing soccer in the rain, or when the field is soaking wet. But the reality is that games do still go on in these conditions. For this reason, it's important that you practice and prepare for competing on wet and rainy days.

Playing on Windy Days

When the wind blows the ball will move faster in one direction and slower in another. The ball will also change its direction, either slightly or dramatically. It all depends on the strength of the wind.

To deal with windy conditions, a goalkeeper must be more patient than usual. He also needs to learn how to estimate the correct direction of the ball before taking off or making a dive.

When winds are high, it's better for the keeper to use his fists to direct the ball towards either sides of the goal. This is a better approach, in these conditions, than attempts at catching the ball.

This is even more important in situations where there are a plenty of opponent's close to the goal line. Just one little misjudgment and an opponent will be ready to pounce.

A strong blowing wind is a good barometer of a goalkeeper's true strength and fitness levels. It takes more effort to jump and dive in blustery conditions than in calm weather. Strong winds essentially make the keeper heavier than he actually is.

As with the rain, you need to become familiar with playing in windy conditions. There will be occasions, when the wind is hard against you, where your saves rely more on potluck than skill or fitness.

When a team is playing with the wind behind them, they ask one thing of their keeper. That is, they encourage him to send long balls and punts toward the opposite side. This can causes the other team's defensive to make mistakes as they prepare to receive the ball.

Why?

Because it will usually end up going further than they had anticipated. As such, the goalkeeper is doing a big favor for his offensive teammates as they get to exploit their opponent's mistakes.

When the wind is on your side, and you know how to use it to best effect, you get to create some serious scoring opportunities.

Playing on Sunny Days

Finally we have sunny days. Whatever the weather condition is, those goalkeepers who have skills for playing in all weathers are the ones who consistently come out on top.

A bright, sunny day might sound ideal but that's not always the case. Two examples of where the sun is against you is if you overheat, or the sun is low and in your eyes.

When the sun blocks the goalkeeper's vision it can sometimes be impossible to make an accurate save from sight alone.

In cases like this, the best chance the keeper has is his experience. In other words, he has to predict the ball's direction.

If he predicts right, by the time the ball does come into view he's in the right spot to catch or deflect it. There are other, less conventional ways to deal with a bright sun too.

During the 2002 FIFA World Cup in South Korea and Japan, a Turkish goalkeeper had his own, unique approach for dealing with the sun.

It was a strange, yet effective method, at least for the Turkish goalkeeper, Rüştü Reçber, it was. Reçber would paint the skin below his eyes with a black ink, or something similar.

He did this so that neither the light of the sun nor the stadium's strong spot lights would distract him or affect his vision too much.

He played just great in that tournament too. In fact, he could have won the Golden Glove Award for his outstanding performance.

It was the German legend, Oliver Kahn, who prevented Reçber getting the Golden Glove. It was unlucky for Reçber that Kahn made the performance of his life in that World Cup, thus snatching this prestigious award for himself.

Still, all was not lost. Reçber went on to win the bronze medal with his national team in that 2002 World Cup, jointly hosted by Korea and Japan.

It doesn't matter what approaches you take to enhance your performance in various weather conditions. As long as it works for you, and doesn't break any rules, then do whatever you need to.

31. Don't Stop Playing Unless You Hear the Referee`s Whistle

Never stop playing or taking action on a ball unless you hear the referee's whistle loud and clear.

In a lot of cases, an attacker from the opposite team will be standing in a position that looks to be offside. The moment this attacker receives the ball the defenders, as well as the goalkeeper, may begin to lose their focus.

They might even stop playing, assuming the ref has seen the error. If he hasn't, they will call out for an offside. But here's the thing: a referee will only call for an offside if he sees it and believes it to be true.

If he didn't see what happened, or he didn't feel it was a violation, then it is game on as usual. He wouldn't call an offside just on the hearsay of a couple of team players.

Imagine the chaos that could cause if it worked. So in the scenario above, you and your team have paused play when the ref didn't blow his whistle.

You assumed he would do, but he didn't, much to your detriment.

The attacker, who everyone was so obsessed about, then goes on to score a goal. These situations are a lot more common than you might think.

To protect yourself from falling into this trap you only need to follow one rule, and that is to KEEP PLAYING. So don't try to raise your hand to get the ref's attention. Don't stop to look at the linesman to see if he has noticed any violation.

And most important of all, don't stop playing in the hope the ref has seen what you have seen.

The only time you stop - the only time - is if you hear the referee`s whistle or see him raise his hand for an offside. If you stop for any other reason, you will likely kick yourself later.

32. Don't Allow Opponents to Distract You - Illegally

Some opponents may try to distract you in the hope that you lose focus. This is most likely when you're playing great and acting as an effective barrier between them and the goal.

Some methods of distraction can be smart. Others might be less tactical and more hostile in nature. For example, they may attempt to trash-talk you by calling you nasty names. Others may go one step further and decide to hit you when the referee`s not looking.

This is more likely if they're getting a thrashing by your side. By hit, I don't mean a physical punch, but more of an accidentally-on-purpose barge and the like. In some cases, though quite rare, an agitated opponent might commit a dangerous foul against you.

I once watched a handball game between France and Egypt in the Handball World Cup. The French, who were playing on their home ground, were behind in the score. It wasn't surprising as the Egyptian keeper was doing a fantastic job at saving most of their shots.

When the French realized he was just too good for them, they resorted to underhanded tactics. This was clearly out of desperation as the clock was ticking away fast. Here's what happened:

One of the French players went on a breakaway, but instead of shooting at the net he went after the keeper instead. He hit the ball as hard as he could, aiming straight at the Egyptian keeper's face. He got him too.

The result was a broken nose, shock, and plenty of pain. Needless to say that this kept him out of action for the final part of the game; the exact result the French hoped for!

This desperate measure was the only way they had to win the game and get to become the champions of the world.

This is wrong, of course, and very unsportsmanlike. It could even be a criminal act if the keeper could prove it was deliberate.

However you look at it, this was an act of pure nastiness. The reason for mentioning it here is because these things happen in most sports, including soccer.

There will always be occasions where someone tries to distract you, but it won't always be legal. Be ready for anything as anything can happen.

Know how you intend to react before a provocation even occurs. If you do this, you will be less likely to take the bait and just press on with the game.

Make sure you inform the referee whenever anyone confronts you with these underhanded distractions. And don't hesitate to tell if the opponent doesn't let up after you ask him to stop.

As a goalkeeper you have special treatment, and the best time to ask for it is when you need it the most.

Once you inform the referee he can then keep his eyes on this player, which means you don't have to. No one likes telling tales, but there are some situations where you have little choice.

There are legal ways to distract an opponent, and these are fine. But we must never tolerate bully-boy tactics on the soccer field. They are no more acceptable here than in a school playground, so make sure you never suffer in silence.

33. Control the Tempo of a Game

As a goalkeeper you must use the privileges the soccer laws bequests you (see below). You need to be particularly mindful of this when playing in tough competitions.

It is not only for your benefit but that of your team too. This is especially important in critical situations. This will include times when your team is under constant attack for long periods. By "long periods" I mean 5, 10 or 15 minutes of continuous attacks by the opposite team.

As the goalkeeper there are certain things you can do to give your team a breather; a little time to catch their breath and recompose themselves.

So if you notice your teammates tiring fast, then you have the ability to help out. There might be other times when the rival side is behind in the score.

Perhaps they're going crazy, doing anything and everything they can to score an equalizer. Desperate situations like this call for desperate measures, on both sides.

This is especially the case when there are only a few minutes to go before the end of the game. Once again, you can fall back on your goalkeeper privileges to help out here.

In these situations, and others like them, your role is to do whatever it takes for you to calm the play down.

It's a powerful thing knowing that you can gain yourself and your team a few moments when necessary. Whether you need the time to waste a minute or two, or to regain your breath and reorganize your side, you the goalie can make it happen.

Goalkeeper's Privileges

OK, let's look at how you might go about using your goalkeeper's privileges. First you need to make sure that you benefit from every ball you catch.

You do this by holding the ball between your arms for a few seconds each time before sending it back into play. Don't forget the six-second rule though.

Once you put the ball back into play, have the players keep it moving with short passes. Make sure the ball stays with those teammates in your own half. Don't pass the ball into the opposite side of the field, unless the situation warrants it.

The other thing you could do to buy a bit of time is play goal kicks. You might also consider indirect free kicks. These would typically result from calling offside on your opponents. The secret here is to not make it look obvious. If you do, then you risk getting a yellow card.

A last thing you could do is to exaggerate any kick, hit or touch you receive from any rival player from the other team.

This way you can waste a few seconds, or minutes even, by claiming you're hurt. That's hurt, not injured. If you scream an injury you might get sent off the field. No, just look hurt to the point where you need a bit of time to recompose yourself, that's all.

This may not sound moral but it's what most goalkeepers do if needs be. If you don't do it, the opposition keeper will do it instead, if he gets the chance.

As you can see, the goalkeeper has certain privileges where he gets to control the tempo of the game. Use these privileges wisely and they will serve you and your team well.

34. Avoid Giving Your Opponents Easy Penalties

Always be aware in one-to-one situations that the opponent might try to trick you. Some players intentionally throw themselves on the ground when the goalkeeper comes out to challenge them.

The trickster then rolls around on the floor and demands a penalty. If the attacker is convincing enough, the referee will count a foul and a penalty on you. He might also give you a yellow card for tripping the player and preventing him from scoring.

Situations like the one above can get even worse if there weren't any of your teammates covering the goal behind you. In this case, the yellow card might become a red. If that happens, the referee will send you off for something you most likely didn't even do.

The only thing you can do to avoid these situations is to be careful not to give the player an opportunity to perform his tricks.

That means you need to be extra careful not to touch the attacking player. If you do, even if it's only a slight brush, he might take advantage of it.

If the opponent is hell-bent on playing his trick anyway, then he will. All you can do in that case is argue in your defense and try to get the ref to see reason.

35. Avoid Sending a Save Back Toward Your Opponent

Whenever you go out of your area to catch a corner or to clear a ball away from your goal line, remember this: Never ever send the ball back toward the middle of the penalty area where your opponents are most likely standing.

Before you try to save or catch a ball, always consider the positions of the opponents. You need to work out where they are standing relative to your goal line.

There's a good reason why you have to be careful in these situations. If you clear the ball away and it arrives at the feet of an opponent, he then has a golden opportunity.

This time, he gets to place that ball into an empty net. If that happens, your strategy to come away from the goal to save the ball becomes a waste of time.

There's little point in saving any ball that is likely to end up back at the feet of a rival attacker. If you can't catch the ball, then you have to try and clear it to safety. Clearing it back in the direction of an opponent is totally unsafe.

The solution is quite a simple one. First, take a quick look around your goal area to see where the opponents are. Second, if you're going to clear the ball away, make sure you direct it to an area that benefits you, not your opponents.

If things are a bit crowded around your goal, at the very least send the ball to where a direct shot at the goal would be difficult.

36. Have Confidence in Yourself

You may be a good height, have a strong, well-toned body, and the ability to play a decent game of soccer. And because of this you may also make it into a good team. But being good is not the same as being great.

The difference between being a good goalkeeper and a great one is often down to one thing - CONFIDENCE! You can have all the physical skills in the world, but you will never become great at goalkeeping if you don't have a strong belief in yourself.

Self-confidence is the one thing that all the great goalkeepers have in common.

The Confidence Ted talk

In one of his TedX talks, Dr. Ivan Joseph spoke about what he looks for in a player. For anyone who doesn't know, Dr. Ivan Joseph is a respected university soccer coach in the USA.

He said that the first and the most important things he looks for in an individual are self-confidence and self-belief.

Anything else is secondary. Whether he accepts a student and awards them scholarship depends on how they perceive themselves.

For Dr. Ivan Joseph, they must have total faith and belief in their ability to succeed. Or at the very least they must have the "potential" to have total faith and belief in their ability to succeed

Dr. Ivan Joseph defines confidence like this:

"It's the skill of believing in one`s ability to perform an act or reach a desired result despite of the odds, the difficulty, or the adversity."

He went on to say that no matter how strong or how fast a player is, these physical features won`t serve him or her well if the belief in one`s self was absent.

He explains his idea with the following quote:

"When we lose sight or lose belief in ourselves, then we will end up achieving nothing."

I recommend you search for his TEDx speech on YouTube. Just type: Dr. Ivan Joseph - The Skill of Self Confidence – TED.

You can measure how strong a team is by the strength of their goalkeeper. This relates to both physical and mental strength. If you look at all the A-Class soccer teams, almost all of them have a strong keeper.

These guys at the top of their game seem to have a special personality. It's a kind of combination between self-confidence and natural leadership.

Look at the greats like Peter Schmeichel, Oliver Kahn and Lev Yashin. All these guys possess a strong belief in themselves.

Some people don't need any help with their confidence. To a few, this state is natural. They are the lucky ones. For the rest, self-confidence is one of those things that could use some work. Some will need to do a lot of work, others only a little.

But most will need to work on this crucial area to some degree. The question is how can you build your self-confidence in a way that helps you to excel as a goalkeeper?

If you have already watched the video I mentioned earlier, you will already know the answer.

For those who haven't seen the video, here is the outline on how to work on your self-confidence. There are actually two approaches to this.

1. Repetition

You first need to identify your mistakes and weak points. This is because they are the problem. It's impossible to apply a solution to anything until you first understand the problem.

OK, so once you have identified your problem areas you need to zoom in and work hard at improving them. If it's a lack of some skill, you have to work over and over until you have improved. When you can do something well you become confident. When you can't, you are insecure and lack confidence.

In the TEDx talk with Dr. Joseph (see above), he gives an example of one of his goalkeepers. This guy, despite being physically capable, had a problem with catching the ball. No matter how hard he tried, the ball would almost always slip through his fingers.

There was nothing wrong with his hands or his eyesight, but the more he tried, the more he failed. What happened was that he had convinced himself that he was useless when it came to catching a soccer ball.

In the wise words of Henry Ford:

"Whether you think you can, or you think you can't, you're right on both counts."

It's all about what you believe to be true. Just as we can excel with the right level of confidence, so we can fail without it. Having the physical potential doesn't help if the brain is not on side.

OK, so in the case of the young goalie above, let's look at how he overcame his inability to catch soccer balls.

Under the instructions of Dr. Joseph, he practiced kicking a ball against a wall and catching it on the rebound, or at least tried to catch it. He did this 350 times a day for eight consecutive months. Repetition was the method here.

So did he make it, did he overcome his belief that he was useless when it came to catching a soccer ball? Well, let's just say he found his confidence and went on to play in Europe; the dream of every young goalkeeper.

For you to duplicate this approach you first find out what you are not so good at. You then get to work at fixing your weak areas using the simple repetition technique. Don't let impatience get the better of you.

Just do the best you can for the agreed training time. Whatever you do, don't tell yourself that you can't do it, or that you're no good. All that kind of thinking will do is hold you back still further. Look for progress my friend, not perfection.

Let's say you are not good at corners, for example. In this case, get someone to send you crosses from different positions and sides of the field. Do it every night if you can, or after finishing your regular training sessions.

Promise to keep at it until you are happy and confident in your ability. It might take two or three months, or it might take six months or even one year. Don't worry about the time. Focus only on the skill.

Tell yourself from the outset that it takes as long as it takes, and then just get on with the task in hand. You might sometimes have a bad day, or a bad few days, where nothing seems to go right.

If this happens, just remind yourself that it's all part of the process. Tell yourself that your improvement is inevitable, despite any setbacks, and it will be.

Whatever area or areas need work, use the repetition technique to zoom in and focus on them. Repetition is the mother of skill. Constant repetition carries conviction. It works, it really does, providing you stick with it.

2. Affirmations

Affirmations are positive statements that describe a desired situation. The general approach is to repeat them over and over. This is often done out loud, until they get impressed on the subconscious mind.

In other words, you repeat them until you believe them to be true.

In your case, these affirmations need to be specific statements. When practiced often they will help you to overcome self-sabotaging, negative thoughts and beliefs.

Muhammad Ali, the greatest boxer of all time once said:

"I am the greatest. I said that before I knew I was."

And this is exactly what you should be telling yourself. Anything less and you will get less.

Belief is something that works both ways, as is beautifully summed up in the Henry Ford quote above. So you are only ever able to excel in something when you believe it's achievable. Likewise, you will never be able to achieve something if you think it's impossible. In other words, you're right on both counts.

So if you believe that you are just average or mediocre and will never be anything other, then you won't be.

What if you don't believe in yourself, what good are positive affirmations then? Well, just because you don't believe you can do a thing, that doesn't mean you can't. It just means you think you can't.

But if you always think that way, then you will never change. In this case you have to fake it till you make it, if that's what it takes. This not only applies to soccer, but to life in general. My advice to anyone is to never knock something new until you try it.

If you're skeptical about positive affirmations working, don't be. After all, if you can't do something, it is most likely because you have convinced yourself you can't. In other words, even though you don't know it, you have been using affirmations all along.

The problem is you've been telling yourself you can't do a thing. This is a negative affirmation. Tell yourself often enough and you believe it.

Well, positive affirmations work in the exact same way. The only difference here is that you're using affirmations for positive reinforcement, not negative.

When building a new belief system, whatever you repeat the most, the subconscious mind eventually considers it to be true.

This is such a simple technique to changing the mindset but it's an effective one nonetheless. All kinds of people use positive affirmations to help change their life for the better. If you want changes in your own belief system you now have the tools to do just that.

Remember that thinking without doing won't help. By that I mean it's no good believing you're great at goal kicks, for example, if you don't then get out there and prove yourself right.

When you believe you can do a thing, then achieving it becomes so much easier. So whatever you do, remember to act on your thoughts. That's positive thoughts, not negative.

Scientists and researchers have tried to explain the phenomenon of the different mindsets. They believe it comes down to two things. One is what they call the Growth Mindset and other the Fix Mindset. Let's look at each of these in turn.

The Growth Mindset

Anyone with a "growth mindset" is positive. They believe they can develop their most basic abilities through dedication and hard work.

They are generally upbeat in their attitude and outlook upon life in general. Those with a growth mindset have within them a genuine love of learning. In essence, they have a resilience that is essential for great accomplishment.

If you look at all the soccer greats you will find that many of them have these qualities. Having a growth mindset creates motivation and productivity. This not only applies to soccer but to all sports, and in business and education.

People with this kind of mindset tend to have good relationships as well. To sum up, people with a growth mindset are happier, healthier and have a real zest for living. They embrace new challenges, knowing that they will come out stronger on the other side.

The Fixed Mindset

People with a "fixed mindset" tend to think more than they act. They do believe in their basic qualities. For example, they believe in their talent, their intelligence, and their physical abilities, etc. But acknowledging their basic qualities is usually where it stops. Despite any beliefs they may have, they do little to develop themselves further.

These types dread failure so they avoid it by no trying. They are of the thinking that talent on its own is enough to succeed and that some people are blessed with certain gifts at birth.

They're wrong, of course, because talent alone is never enough to succeed at anything. Yet so fixed is their belief that it's hard to convince them otherwise.

These types of folks are inflexible. You've heard the saying, "Stuck in their ways." Well, that is typical of a fixed mindset personality. So people with this mindset belong in the "all talk and no action" category.

They usually have a lowly opinion of themselves in general, even though they might not voice it out loud. People with this mindset often worry about their traits. With a fixed mindset it's hard to deal with criticism, even when it's constructive. In short, a fixed mindset suggests limited negative thinking patterns.

If you can identify with the fixed mindset then don't get too despondent. You can change your mindset through various exercises. There have been entire books written about this, but to sum it up in brief, here is the crux of what you need to do to shift from a negative fixed mindset to a positive growth mindset.

Listen to Your Fixed Mindset Voice

Learn to listen to your fixed mindset "voice." This is the voice that tells you that something is impossible. It is the voice that says you can't do a thing. It then justifies itself by having you come up with a 101 reasons why this is true.

So the first thing to do is to recognize this voice. Understand that YOU are not your mind. Your mind is a part of who you are, just like any other body part. That means you can learn to control it.

Acknowledge Your Choices

The second thing to do, once you have recognized your inner voice, is to acknowledge that you have choices. So far you have chosen to believe all that is negative. It is something that you subconsciously chose to believe based on your mindset.

You can now consciously choose not to believe your fixed-mindset anymore. From today you get to choose to develop your growth-mindset. Whenever your inner voice tells you, "No, you can't," turn things around by saying, "Oh yes I can."

Listen, Learn and Act

Finally, practice at hearing both voices, fixed and growth. Get used to taking (choosing) the growth mindset action. For example, say you're having a tough time diving.

The old fixed mindset might tell you that it's because you've reached the limits of your potential. It tells you that this is as good as you're likely to get, so QUIT trying.

And your growth mindset tells you there's lots of room for improvement. It suggests you look at other ways to develop, and maybe you could ask for help from those more experienced. You choose to listen to the growth mindset and take fresh action.

To begin with, your fixed mindset will be your default way of thinking. You will have to counteract it by forcing the growth mindset to take part. What you're doing here is trying to wake up the growth mindset.

Just start by giving yourself alternative options. These are usually the total opposite to what the fixed mindset suggests. So if your fixed mindset says, "No, you can't," replace that with "Yes I can, and I will." I'm sure you get the idea.

Providing you take action on the positive thoughts, your growth mindset will take over control from the fixed. It will likely take some time, so the sooner you start on this, the quicker you get to transform.

If you need more help, there are plenty of good books and articles online that you can use to help guide you in the process.

37. Work on Your Reflexes

Your reflexes are nerve signal-induced muscular reactions that react to external stimuli. In simpler language, they are what signal you to take immediate action, and with little or no conscious thought.

Reflexes help you to save yourself from hurt or injury. Even though the reflex is spontaneous, you still act in a way that best suits the situation. The faster your reflexes are, the better the outcome of your action will be.

A goalkeeper has to always prepare for the unexpected. Balls can, and quite often do, come at him when he isn't expecting them.

There are many situations in soccer where erratic, fast, and crazy things just happen. Say you turn around and see a soccer ball suddenly flying toward your head at high speed.

If you weren't expecting it, your brain sends a signal to your hand to block that ball before it hits you hard in the face.

Whether you succeed or not depends on how fast your reflexes are. Having quick reflexes is the most important aspect for good goalkeeping, for obvious reasons.

We all have reflex actions, some fast, others not so quick. But we're not stuck with what we've got. You can develop your reflexes just like you can develop your muscles. The best goalkeepers all work hard to improve their reflexes. This is something you will also want to do.

Just a second too late in a save attempt can mean a lost goal. A goalkeeper with quick reflexes can stop rebounds and perform lightning-fast reaction saves.

He is especially good with low shots and on second-chance shots. How fast a goalkeeper reacts to a save is an important stat to note for any club on the lookout for a new goalie.

These guys are worth their weight in gold to any team. Good reflexes turn goalkeepers into match savers. In short, reflexes can make or break a goalkeeper depending on his reaction time. Some examples of goalies with fast reflexes include: The Spaniard Iker Casillas, Belgian Thibaut Courtois, and the German Manuel Neuer.

How to Develop Your Reflexes

What I will show you here are some drills that you can use to improve your reflexes. The intensity of the training is up to you.

I do recommend, however, that you allow ample time to work on these exercises. Having great reflex actions is crucial if you want to become a highly sought after goalkeeper.

Drill 1:

This drill is ideal for helping you to deal with breakaways. It's also useful for one-to-one situations. If you get good at this, you'll become a master at catching any ball that comes at you above the shoulders.

For this drill you need a hockey goal and someone to assist you. The assistant sends your balls just above your shoulder level. Your aim is to move your shoulders as fast and as high as possible to save the balls.

Drill 2:

This drill is a good one for developing your reflexes. You will also need someone to help you train with this exercise too.

OK, to perform this drill your assistant has to stand behind you, on a box or something. He needs to stand taller than you for this to work. Once in position, he begins to throw balls to your right and your left side. Your job is to quickly figure out the direction of the ball and then attempt to save it before it reaches the ground.

The reason your assistant throws the balls from behind is so that you don't know what direction they will appear from next. This is the point. It is why you need quick reflexes, so that you can act fast and save the ball before it lands.

Drill 3:

In this drill you will need three others to help you.

Each of the three assistants will stand in different positions inside the penalty area.

Their only job is to fire fast balls at you from different locations. They can do this either by foot (low balls) or by hands (high balls). The idea is for you to be in continuous motion and maintain good focus and use quick reflexes.

The important part of this drill is that you don't know who will be shooting next. That means you don't get to decide whose turn it is. This is something the assistants can arrange between themselves, but you mustn't know.

This is an excellent exercise for developing your reflex times. The exercise needs to be fast and relentless. It won't hurt to take things a little slower until you get used to it though. Yes, you need to work hard, but no, it's not a lesson in torture.

Drill 4:

In this drill you will have your back to your assistant. He then starts to throw high and low balls at you in different directions, at a moderate speed.

Your job here is to turn around, latch your focus on the ball, and attempt to catch it the second he releases it. You won't know its direction which means you have to act real fast.

Drill 5:

This is a fun drill. To perform this you and your assistant begin by passing the ball between yourselves in a casual way. After a while, and unbeknown to you, he fires a shot instead of an easy pass.

This shot should be at ground level to get the most gain from this drill. You will have to move fast, going from the standing position to a dive to the ground.

Drill 6:

This drill is to help you deal with balls played at ground level (just like drill 5). Here you will be standing in the middle, between a wide wooden box and an assistant. Keep in mind that the box should be in front of you and your assistant behind.

Once the drill starts, the assistant shoots the ball toward the wooden box. Your job is to react to the ball that deflects from that box at your goal.

Drill 7:

For this drill your assistant will arm himself with a tennis racket and a bunch of tennis balls. The job of the assistant is to bounce the tennis balls off the ground or directly toward you using the racket. The idea behind this exercise is to challenge you at saving fast balls.

This is an important drill for developing the speed of your reflexes. As before, start as slow as you need to, just until you get used to it. Then, as soon as you are ready, up the pace so that you get to really challenge yourself.

38. Avoid Surrendering to the Jeering Fans

There may be times when you experience verbal hostility from the other team's fans. The chance of this always increases in away games. It is not acceptable behavior, but it still happens nonetheless.

That means it's something you have to learn to deal with. It's better to know about this now, and learn how to cope with it, before you get to play to bigger crowds.

When it first happens it can be uncomfortable to say the least. Hostile chants from rival fans can be more unpleasant for goalkeepers than field players.

This is because the keeper is often out there alone and exposed. It's even worse when the hecklings come as he waits around for some action. The way you react, or not, as the case may be, determines how you deal with these situations.

In times like these you need to do two things. The first is to develop the skin of a Rhinoceros, and the second is to learn how to turn a deaf ear.

Don't ever take the bait because that's what the hecklers want you to do. Any time you react on an emotional level, you lose some focus.

By overacting to verbal hostility you are also playing right into the hands of the tormentors. I say NEVER give them that satisfaction. OK, let's take a look at what you can do to lessen the effect of these uncomfortable moments.

Your response is simple. That is, it's simple in theory but a little harder in practice. It depends how nasty the jeering is at you. But you can't let this bad behavior affect your game.

So the only way to approach any hostility is either by paying no attention to any of it, or with a smile and calm stance. Neither of these responses are what your intimidators expects. That means they will soon give up when their nastiness backfires on them.

Learning how to turn a blind eye and a deaf ear is all part of your mental game. If you find it difficult, then you have work at getting better at it, just like with any other skill.

Just know that as unpleasant as jeering is, it's rarely personal. In soccer, anyone playing on the side, e.g. left back, right winger, or anyone playing corner kicks, all experience some verbal abuse.

It's not nice, but it's the way things are. So if you're a bit on the sensitive side right now, start to work on this sooner rather than later. This way, at least you will be ready for when it happens, and it will.

Hostile Chants from Your Own Fans

It's a sad fact but there will be occasions when a goalie experiences hostility from his fans. One example might be if he happens to make a stupid mistake that results in a silly goal. This is a good excuse to become the best keeper you can be. The better you are, the fewer mistakes you will make, especially silly ones.

Note I say "silly goal" here. Fans are not so ruthless that they will give you grief for letting in an impressive goal. If a striker from the rival side scores in a spectacular fashion, then so be it. No one likes to see their team defeated, of course.

But every genuine soccer fan respects an impressive goal from either side. But a lost goal because of a lack of concentration, or a silly slip, well, that's not so forgiving.

Remember, keeping a cool head while playing in goal is the best weapon you have against jeering fans. It's also the best way for you to maintain focus and continue to play consistently well.

39. Practice Meditation Before Game Day

If I told you that a lot of successful soccer players meditate, you might think I was joking. I'm not. Many players, and that includes goalkeepers, attribute their calmness and high state of focus to meditation.

Some may use other mindfulness routines too. The point is they all learn the art of stillness and inner calm. They do this for no other reason than it works, and it works well.

Former Dutch player Dennis Bergkamp, and Denmark's Peter Schmeichel, both said they meditation. They not only mediated once, but twice on the night before a big game.

Other Reasons to Meditate

Science has shown that meditation has a number of positive benefits. It boosts self-confidence, self-esteem, and general wellbeing. It also increases optimism and self-awareness. Some ADHD sufferers have also found advantages in meditation.

For thousands of years, meditators have claimed the many benefits for their ancient practice. But it has only been in recent times that The West has embraced this old practice from The East.

As a goalkeeper meditation will enhance your ability to make critical decisions. It will also help you to manage distractions and feel in better control more generally.

If it all sounds a bit too "spiritual" for you, and not really your thing, then try to view it in a different way. Look at meditation as nothing more than sitting still in a quiet space for a set period of time.

After all, that's what it is, in its most basic form at least. Set aside 15-30 minutes a day for a week, and at the same time each day. You will know by the end of your seven day trial whether you want to carry on or not.

How to Meditate

- Wear something loose-fitting and comfortable.
- Find a calm space to practice.

- Switch off your mobile and any other distracting devices.
- Get into a comfortable sitting position with your feet resting flat on the floor.
- Close your eyes and focus on your breath, breathing in through your nose and out through the mouth.
- Stay put for the time you have set aside.

You will have all kinds of thoughts and distractions when you first start to meditate. This is quite normal, so don't think you're failing if you find it hard to still the mind at first.

Let any thoughts come and go from your mind.

Don't try to control them or get into internal conversations. Just allow them to happen. Your aim here is to just watch your thoughts as an outside observer.

OK, so the above guide is the most basic level of meditation. If you feel you want to get deeper into this there is a plethora of great advice and information on the web.

40. Affect Other Players with Your Performance

The performance of a goalkeeper, good or bad, has an effect on all players. So how does this happen? When the goalie is doing a great job he inspires courage and boosts moral within his teammates.

For example, he makes outstanding saves and keeps all kinds of balls out of his goal. His defensive players are particularly pleased with his performance.

If he's having a bad day and letting in plenty of goals, especially easy ones, then the reverse is true. In this case the field players become discouraged and moral starts to falter.

Imagine your team is giving an aggressive opponent a real run for their money. Your field players are all performing well, even though the odds are against them. Likewise, despite there being plenty of shots at you, you still manage to keep your goal safe.

Regardless of being the underdogs in this game, the team morale is high. You are all feeding off each other's outstanding performances. In this situation it's all good. You even have a fighting chance to win.

Now let's change the situation a bit. Your teammates still start off strong and play a blinding game out on the field. And let's say you're the only weak link in the chain on this day. Almost every attack at your goal succeeds for the opponents.

The longer this goes on for, the more despondent the other players become. Now team moral begins to plummet. The performance of your side starts to falter as they see their chances destroyed at your door.

It's understandable how you can affect the team either way, depending on your own performance. As you can see, there's always a lot of pressure on the goalkeeper to save the day. You have the ability to inspire greatness in your teammates and get them motivated.

No one can expect you to save every goal. But what they should be able to reply on is consistency in your style. Even if your team is having a bad run, you cannot look downbeat or defeated. The way you perform also relates to the way you act more generally.

It Ain't over till the Fat Lady Sings

As the goalkeeper, you must remain positive and motivational up until the final whistle. You have to embrace the "It ain't over till the fat lady sings" approach to any competition.

This simple colloquialism means one should not presume to know the outcome of an event that is still in progress. We've all seen it before. A losing side begins to look like losers before they're even halfway through.

Their faces and body language say it all. You can tell that they have accepted defeat even though there's enough time left to make a comeback. A lot of this has to do with how their goalkeeper performs, acts, and communicates.

Play every game like your life depended on it. Stay fired up right till the end, even if you're getting a thrashing from the rival side.

Walk off the field knowing you did the best possible job you could have done under the circumstances. As long as you can hold your head up high after a defeat, confidence and moral will remain intact.

41. Do Not Think About Getting Hurt

In many situations, the keeper fears going out from his goal. He fears that a certain move or a certain dive might result in a physical injury. Sometimes he's just worried about getting hurt or bruised. This 'fear' is even more likely to materialize if the opponents are aggressive in their attacks.

Of course it's important to prevent injury whenever you can. What you mustn't do though, is allow the "potential" of injury to occupy your thoughts too much. If you let the fear of getting hurt govern the way you play in goal, two things happen. The first is that you end up missing opportunities. The second is that you begin to underperform. Both of these become the inevitable consequence of overcautious behavior.

It is quite normal for all human beings to feel afraid of pain and injury. Our brains are programmed to avoid danger; it's our natural defense mechanism. The process of exaggerating and overreacting to situations are methods our minds use to keep us safe.

But when we allow fear to run rampant it becomes a problem. This can happen after a nasty attack or an injury that hurt like crazy.

In situations like these, we return to our position with more fear and caution than we had previously. And the more we fear, the more fearful we become. Oftentimes, these fears are not as real as we make them up to be.

False Evidence Appearing Real

You can look at F.E.A.R. as an acronym for False Evidence Appearing Real. What that means is we can cook things up in our heads that are not actual, or nowhere near as tangible as we make them up to be.

What I mean by this is that there's no definite threat of immediate physical danger. If we just step back and think about a situation in a rational way, we may actually see that our F.E.A.R. is an illusion.

Put another way, it is something we have fabricated in our own minds, and because of that we pretend it's real.

As a goalkeeper, you must not allow fear to occupy too much of your conscious thoughts. Instead, limit this to a specific set of situations where it's warranted. Fear has its place but it needs to be healthy fear, and kept in perspective.

Many keepers develop healthy fears for certain types of plays. But when fear gets misconstrued it becomes a problem. Let's take a look at a real-world example. In this case we will use the Petr Čech incident to illustrate.

Petr Čech is the leading goalkeeper for Arsenal and the Czech national team. Before playing for Arsenal he was the best goalkeeper in the history of Chelsea. He became their legendary player, helping them to win 15 different trophies. This included one UEFA Champions league in the year 2012.

In the game against Reading, on 14 October, 2006, Cech sustained a serious head injury. He collided with midfielder Stephen Hunt inside Chelsea's penalty area. This was within the first minute of the game. He recovered, but doctors later reported the accident almost cost Čech his life.

Despite great performances with Chelsea, Čech became more cautious after his near fatal accident. This is most notable when he has to deal with high balls.

He still knows how to catch a high ball, he hasn't lost that ability. But he now comes out of his goal to catch crosses less often than he did before he was injured.

Čech is still a great goalkeeper though. He wouldn't be playing in professional soccer if he wasn't. But he's not quite the man he once was. This is because he now holds on to the fear of a repeat accident, just like the one that almost cost him his life.

Some keepers become afraid of injures to the face, nose or between their legs in particular. You might see this as a justifiable fear, and one that keeps them safe.

But with fear comes caution and with caution comes some degree of underperformance. So are such fears justified? The answer would be yes, but only if goalkeepers sustained lots of injures in these areas, but they don't.

So you need to do a little research here and look at some facts. Find out which fears are healthy. As you do this you also get to learn which fears are overblown.

Once you have fear put into some sort of perspective your mindset should change for the better. Hopefully now you have less fear and more bravery in all areas of your game.

Bravery will see you saving many more goals than fear and caution. And the braver you are the more confident you become in your ability as a goalkeeper. A great goalie is tough, physically and mentally. He has to be able to leap, catch and kick with a degree of fearlessness.

If you are already playing in goal then you are already brave. The question you need to ask yourself is am I brave enough. Developing bravery is more to do with psychology than physical ability.

Here are a few pointers that might help you put the fear thing into some kind of perspective:

The first thing you need to know is that outfield players can be just as afraid as you are when coming entering your goal area. Another thing to consider is that injuries are part of the game. Nobody wants to get injured, but sometimes they do. This applies to all players, not only goalkeepers, so you're all in this together.

And finally, we die if we worry and we die if we don't. So why worry? Worrying about suffering a "rare" injury and wrapping yourself in cotton wool takes the "fun" out of goalkeeping.

And without the fun element, there is no point. Just be mindful of the fact that thinking will never overcome fear, but action will.

"The only thing we have to fear is fear itself." ~ Franklin D. Roosevelt

42. Use Video to Record Yourself

Get into the habit of having someone record your performance. This is not so much for seeing what you're doing right, but what you're doing wrong. Things will quite often show up on video that you or others were unable to spot otherwise.

With video you get to pause, rewind, and replay as often as you like. Needless to say that video is an invaluable tool for any goalkeeper. It can help you identify areas of your game that could use some real improvements.

Once you have some recordings I suggest you spend at least one day every week viewing the footage. What you need to do is identify any notable mistakes.

The ones you will want to take most notice of are those that recur. The idea is to then plan various drills and exercises to correct these mistakes. Also look for any weaknesses in general, and then get to work at strengthening any you come across.

Too many young goalkeepers fail to reach their true potential. They think they're doing well, but in reality they still fall short in a lot of areas, but they can't see it. Video can though.

All kinds of mistakes show up on camera. You get to see things that are not always obvious when watching the live performance. For example, you might identify bad footwork, rushing in with dives, lazy take-offs, etc.

The first time I used video to record my performance I couldn't believe what I saw. I noticed how I was not reading the game too well.

I also saw how I was rushing in with decisions and plays when it wasn't really necessary. It all comes out on film once you start to look carefully at the footage.

Try to be consistent with using video. Look at it as a crucial tool for your development because that's what it is.

If you do this, you will become ten times better than the keeper you are today. Video is also something that helps develop the growth mindset that we looked at earlier in the book.

If you happen to spot a lot of mistakes and weak points in your goalkeeping, don't let it put you off. This is the whole point of recording your games. As I mentioned earlier, you can't apply a solution until you first identify the problem.

Regardless of what flaws you find, or how many mistakes you identify, just be grateful for the discovery. If you didn't find these things out then you wouldn't be able to fix them. Goalkeepers who are consistent at developing their skills are those who become great.

It's a fact that many goalkeepers play for years and keep repeating a bad technique or a shabby move. And because they don't use video, most never get to know about their more latent flaws. This is something that doesn't have to apply to you, not now that you know the importance of video.

Who Should Film My Performance?

It's crucial that the person recording you knows what it is they need to be filming. It's also important that they know how to use the camera to best effect.

You want to take this footage serious, so make sure you get the best results that you can. Explain to the one doing the recording how you want them to film you.

It will be even better if that person is familiar with soccer and good goalkeeping. This way they will need less direct input from you.

The first video might be a bit hit and miss, but use it to learn from. The important thing you want to be mindful of here is to film at the right positions and from the best angles.

43. Warm up Properly

As you enter the game, your body should be in a state of physical readiness. That means you need to be able to perform a dive or a full body stretch from the off, and with a reduced risk of hurt or injury. This can only happen if you have warmed up before the game.

What you can't do is walk into a game unprepared. You don't have that luxury I'm afraid. It doesn't matter how young or how fit you are, the body still needs to warm up before the real action begins.

The way for a goalie to warm up is to practice all types of balls that he thinks he will face during the competition. He does this at a comfortable pace, just so that he limbers up enough in preparation for the game.

So you will want to warm up with short passes, long passes, and punts, etc. Be sure to use both your left and right legs as you prepare.

Also work with crosses played from different parts of the field. Change the ball speeds too, and have someone fire shots at both the near and far posts.

Do a few high jumps to catch a ball while bending one knee. Besides all these, you will have to practice a few dives too.

Most warm up sessions also include a light jog. You coach will guide you on exactly what he wants you to include in your warm up. The most important thing is that you heed his advice and take the pre-game warm-up serious.

In a game between FC Bayern and FC Hoffenheim, Manuel Neuer conceded a goal in the eighth second. This was the fastest goal in the history of the Bundesliga and scored by Kevin Volland.

It most likely happened because Neuer and his defenders were not adequately prepared. It's impossible for any keeper or field player to be at their best if they skip or skimp on the pre-game warm-up.

A good physical soccer warm has to meet two important objectives. The first is to decrease the risk of injury.

The second is to increase ability levels. When you warm up properly you improve your agility, skill, power and overall functionality.

You are a bundle of energy, ready for any action that comes your way. When you fail to warm up properly, the opposite is true.

To summarize this chapter:

Warming up allows you to perform at your absolute best. It also means you have a much lesser risk of strains, sprains and muscle tears.

All these common types of injury are avoidable by doing a full pre-game warm-up. Or at least the probability of injuries occurring becomes much less after a good warm up session.

Your muscles also produce energy faster when they are warm. The benefit of warm muscles is that you have more speed and power at the start of the game.

Those who haven't warmed up, or skimped on their warm up, have to wait a while for their muscles to get warm.

Warming up also increases your ability to perform complex skills and movements with more accuracy and precision.

As you can see, there is everything to gain by doing a proper pre-game warm-up and everything to lose if you don't.

44. Know How to Shoot a Penalty

There will always be times when your team has to play in a penalty shootout. There will also be times when the two teams fail to finish the game from the first five penalties.

When that happens the shootout continues until the tenth or the eleventh penalty. In this situation, you may find yourself forced to take a penalty, even though you might not be good at it. This is one of the soccer rules so there is no way out of it.

It is therefore a good idea that you know how shoot at a goal. This way, if the time comes for you to take a penalty, at least you can proceed with confidence. So you should include taking penalty shots in your regular soccer training. Let's look at how to best practice this skill.

I would suggest you focus on only one penalty style. Practice it a lot, say 100, 200, or 500 times. Just keep going until you get to master it. In general, there is a reason why goalkeepers only work at perfecting one type of penalty kick.

Players like Cristiano Ronaldo or Lionel Messi take a lot of penalties for their teams. Because of this, all the top professional European goalkeepers study these guys intensively. If Ronaldo and Messi never changed their style they would become too predictable. It would mean the pro keepers had a better chance of saving their shots.

But Ronaldo and Messi know that goalkeepers study them all the time. Because of this they have no choice but to be unpredictable. What they do is practice different types of penalties to deal with different keepers.

They might fire a ball at one of the top corners or at the far bottom. Or they may play a Panenka (a volleyed penalty placed in the middle of the goal). The point is the keeper won't know until it happens.

Things are different for you though. You rarely take a penalty. Because of this, you don't need to practice all the various shots.

This is just as well because you have more important goalkeeping skills to work on and maintain. So for you, just practice one style of shot. This way you have something to use if and when you need to take a penalty for your side.

Here's what I suggest:

Practice by aiming your penalty at one place.

Develop it into a lethal shot. Keep at it over and over until you get good (see chapter 36, the section on the power of repetition).

Pick a side, it doesn't matter which one. Practice firing the ball toward the top corner of your chosen side. This is the place where keepers most likely fail to save a penalty.

The Chilean midfielder, Arturo Vidal, is one of the most successful penalty takers in European soccer right now.

He rarely fails to score a penalty when he places the ball in one of the top corners of a goal. Most of his penalties are lethal and reach the net regardless of how great the keeper might be at saving.

To summarize this chapter:

There may be times when you, the goalkeeper, have to take a penalty. This can happen if the teams fail to finish the game from the first five penalties of a penalty shootout.

Save yourself from embarrassment and master one style of penalty kick so that you are always prepared. Your best option is to work on one of the two top corners.

That's it Folks…

You now have everything you need to know about great goalkeeping and what makes a brilliant goalkeeper as good as he is. Now it's time for a final word of advice. My word is simple and short. In fact, I can sum it up in a single phrase, which is this: Take Action.

It's important to understand that if you don't take action then nothing will ever change. Or if you do take action, yet find that you're not improving, something isn't working.

In this case you have to study your game and see where you can apply new action. Whatever you do, don't keep doing the same thing over and over hoping for different results. It just won't happen. Or as another famous quote from Henry Ford goes;

"If you always do what you've always done, you'll always get what you've always got."

Making Sacrifices

When you take action based on the guidance and suggestions outlined in this book, you will get better. This I can guarantee. How good you get depends on a few factors.

The most important thing you must have is a genuine desire to improve. This requires patience, persistence, and a willingness to make some sacrifices. The difference between a good goalie and a great one is contingent on how serious he is about this #1 position.

Those who want to make it to the top will likely need to cut out, or at least cut down on some of the things they love the most.

I'm talking about favorite foods and various social events here. There's no place for partying, or wine, or women, or all-night binges during the soccer season.

It won't be easy preparing yourself for greatness, but it should still be a lot of fun all the same. This is because of your love for the game and your desire to succeed. Think BIG and never let anyone or anything crush your dreams.

Every single goalkeeper who you know the name of – even the most mediocre of them – has taken lots of action to reach his objectives. For you to succeed you have to believe you are better than everyone else who plays in goal.

Okay, so that might not be true right now, so you have to tell yourself that you can be better than they are. In other words, you have the potential. All these great keepers are human beings, just like you.

Not super human or supermen, just guys that committed themselves to their position. One day they woke up and made a conscious decision to become great and so they did. Be the one.

And finally…

Finally, don't put this book away and forget about it. This is not a novel that you read once and then pass on to someone else. This is a source of great reference. Or as I like to look at it, this is your 'Goalkeeper's Bible.'

Whenever you need to work on some areas of your goalkeeping, find the section in this book which talks about it.

Revisiting different parts of this book is a great way to refresh your mind. Furthermore, as you progress with your development you will pick up different things in this book on the second, third, or fourth read.

Know that hard work, not talent, is the key to getting ahead. Talent alone is useless unless you work hard to reach your goals.

You must also know the difference between working hard and flogging yourself half to death. To work hard means to be consistent, determined and focused, but it also requires you to be smart.

So it's smart to include some balance into your schedule. This means understanding your limits. It's important to know when to take a break and step back sometimes.

Too much of anything is a bad thing. Life is for living, in all its aspects, so remember to live life a little between your training commitments.

Good Luck.

About The Author

Mirsad writes all of his books in a unique style, constantly drawing connections between his past experiences and his reader's goals.

This unique approach means that you can avoid undergoing the same injuries, frustrations, and setbacks that he himself has endured over the years.

He can't produce the results for you, but what he can do is promise that you WILL reach your goals - guaranteed – providing you follow his tips and advice exactly as he outlines them in his books.